DREAMS IN OLD NORSE LITERATURE AND THEIR AFFINITIES IN FOLKLORE

T0370912

DREAMS

IN OLD NORSE LITERATURE AND
THEIR AFFINITIES IN FOLKLORE

With an Appendix containing the Icelandic
Texts and Translations by

GEORGIA DUNHAM KELCHNER

Ph.D. (Cantab.)

CAMBRIDGE
AT THE UNIVERSITY PRESS
1935

CAMBRIDGE UNIVERSITY PRESS
Cambridge, New York, Melbourne, Madrid, Cape Town,
Singapore, São Paulo, Delhi, Mexico City

Cambridge University Press
The Edinburgh Building, Cambridge CB2 8RU, UK

Published in the United States of America by Cambridge University Press, New York

www.cambridge.org
Information on this title: www.cambridge.org/9781107620223

First published 1935
First paperback edition 2013

A catalogue record for this publication is available from the British Library

ISBN 978-1-107-62022-3 Paperback

CONTENTS

PREFACE

This book is the outcome of seven years spent in research as a student of Girton College. My preliminary studies in the Icelandic language and the bulk of my investigation into Old Norse literature and folklore were carried on under the direction of Dame Bertha S. Phillpotts, D.B.E., Litt.D., to whose ever ready guidance and sympathetic understanding I owe more than I am able to express. For the planning of my work and for its substance I alone am responsible.

My thanks are due to the Syndics of the University Press for undertaking its publication, and to members of the staff for their unfailing care and skill.

Finally, it would be impossible for me to measure the share played in the writing of my book by my friend and fellow-worker, Miss Olava Ørbeck, without whose partnership, from beginning to end, it could never have been wrought.

G. D. K.

CAMBRIDGE
August, 1934

ABBREVIATIONS

Fms.	= Fornmannasögur.
Fas.	= Fornaldarsögur Norðrlanda.
Bks.	= Biskupasögur.
Fj. Ísl. Þættir	= Fjörutíu Íslendinga-Þættir.

Note. In Chapters I and II anglicised forms of proper names have been used, in subsequent chapters the Icelandic forms are given.

Chapter I

INTRODUCTORY

T̶w o chief facts give the dreams in Old Norse literature outstanding importance: Firstly, they are the only dreams of the heathen Teutonic people on record. Secondly, they include a proportion of Christian dreams making their way among the people after the coming of the new faith. The object of this study is to examine these dreams and to trace their affinities in folklore.

The term Old Norse literature covers the Elder and Younger Eddas, the Prose Saga and Skaldic poetry. Of these, the Younger or Prose Edda, as befits a manual for poets, largely re-states and re-interprets the lore of the Elder Edda,[1] and most of the Skaldic poetry is embodied in the text of the Sagas. The Elder Edda and the Prose Saga, taken together, thus virtually represent the whole field of our literature.

The Elder Edda is a collection of poems by anonymous authors, most of them probably Norwegian, some Icelandic.[2] It is concerned with the early mythology and cosmogony of the Norsemen, and with their heroic tradition, some of native and some of foreign origin. There is some difference of opinion as to the dating of these poems, but the view now most generally held places the majority of them in the tenth, some in the eleventh, and perhaps one in the twelfth century, while some stanza groups in the oldest poems may go back as far as A.D. 600.[3]

---

[1] It also preserves some material which would otherwise have been lost.

[2] One has been assigned to Greenland, and another shows Celtic affinities and may have originated in a Norse Settlement in Britain or Ireland. (*Edda and Saga*, by B. S. Phillpotts, p. 21.)

[3] *Ibid.*

The Sagas are prose stories of various types for which Icelanders, most of them anonymous, are almost exclusively responsible; they rest for the most part on historical or romantic tradition, plus a proportion of contemporary history on the one hand and of fiction on the other. Under the general designation of history, traditional and actual, are included the earlier, or classical, Sagas on the Great Families of Iceland, the Sagas on the Kings of Norway and Denmark, on the Earls of Orkney, and on the Men of the Faroes; in the collection of Sagas centred about the powerful Sturlung family of Iceland we find accounts of contemporary events based on personal experience or intimate knowledge. Iceland's ecclesiastical history is recorded in the Sagas on her Bishops. Quasi-historical tales, some of them so convincing as to have been mistaken for history, are represented by the later Icelandic Family Sagas and by the fictitious Sagas modelled on the old Family ones. In the domain of legend there are the Sagas on the earliest heroes of Scandinavia, and those dealing with foreign heroes and resting upon foreign tradition. The historical Sagas deal chiefly with events from after the first quarter of the ninth century until toward the end of the thirteenth. The work of putting the Sagas into writing may be roughly described as starting with Ari Frodi Thorgilsson, c. 1120–30, reaching its climax in the years 1170–1230, and entering the stage of compilation and interpolation toward the end of the thirteenth century, to continue through the fourteenth and fifteenth (and even into the sixteenth) centuries in an ever-increasing retreat from the trustworthy tradition of earlier times.

Skaldic (or Court) poetry, that occasional verse of which so much is incorporated in the Sagas, is concerned with historical persons and events, and is usually by known Norwegian and Icelandic authors.[1] The period during which it was composed runs from the beginning of the ninth century to well past the middle of the fourteenth, the Golden Age

[1] Some poets of Greenland and the Orkneys included.

coming to an end about 1100.[1] The term Skaldic embraces all the Old Norwegian and Icelandic poetry which is not included in the Elder Edda.

Dreams are a prominent feature throughout this literature; indeed, it has been estimated that no less than five hundred and thirty dream references are to be found, a proportion greater than that in Middle English.[2] They form an integral part of the works of poetry and prose in which they appear, and their function within the more or less perfectly unified framework which these represent is often well defined and highly significant. Tradition records the occurrence of these dreams as matters of fact, and their value is considerably enhanced through their being supposed to be true.

If we ask how it came about that both heathen and Christian dreams have a place here, we shall find that the answer is closely bound up with the date of the introduction of Christianity in the North. Probably no part of Old Norse literature was written down before something like one hundred and fifty to two hundred years had passed since Christianity was legally established in Iceland in 1000, and King Olaf Tryggvason introduced the new faith into Norway during his short but vigorous reign, 995–1000. Nevertheless, in spite of possible slight traces of Christian influence in some of the later poems, the Elder Edda is essentially heathen. We may expect this to be true also of the legendary Sagas on mythological heroes, but the case of the historical Sagas is somewhat different. These may be divided into three groups, those which deal exclusively with the heathen period, those which cover years in both the heathen and Christian periods, and those which relate entirely to the Christian period. Sagas resting wholly or in part on historical tradition handed down by word of mouth from heathen times, in some instances for more than three hundred years,

---

[1] Finnur Jónsson, *Den Oldnorske og Oldislandske Litteraturs Historie*, Vol. I, p. 356.

[2] E. C. Ehrensperger, P.M.L.A. March, 1931, pp. 80–9.

were put into writing by Christian scribes, compilers and authors at a time when it may seem to us that pre-Christian memories and ideas might already have faded into the background. That so much concerning the early life and thought of the North is known to us is a tribute at once to the purity and freshness of the tradition on which the records are based, and to the tolerance of the Young Icelandic Church which, at least throughout the eleventh century, exerted very little influence on ordinary secular life, and among whose priests and monks many compilers and writers of Sagas were numbered. The dreams in Old Norse literature, conditioned by such a combination of factors, are likely to offer interesting material to the student from various points of view. We shall learn, as our subject unfolds, something of what they have to tell us of the history and evolution of tradition.

In folklore (which Lewis Spence defines as 'the study of primitive religion and customs still practised'[1]) we see the further development of these dreams, and it should not surprise us to find that they have undergone certain changes here. Some types of dream common in Old Norse literature tend to disappear in folklore, while others are modified and appear in a new form; on the other hand, dream types to be reckoned with in folklore may be rare in, or even foreign to, Old Norse literature. In any judgment of the significance of the differences involved, however, the special and particularized nature of the subject matter of our literature, confined in large measure to the affairs and activities of the royal and the mighty, must be taken into account. That is to say, when a dream type is found in folklore which has no counterpart in Old Norse literature the question will arise as to how much this depends on actual evolution and change in dream thought, and how much on such selection as the exigencies of Saga building may be responsible for. But if the absence of folklore types of dream within the limits of Edda and Saga fails to give conclusive proof of their novelty in folk-

---

[1] *An Introduction to Mythology*, p. 221. For further definitions of folklore, see *ibid.* pp. 222–3.

lore, it is all the more important that we should step warily in denying the interrelation of even what may seem sharply divergent types of dream in Old Norse literature and folk-lore respectively. Subtle and varied as well as strong and far-reaching, we shall see by how many links of affinity the dreams of our mediæval literature are bound to those still current in folklore of the present day.

Chapter II

HISTORICAL BACKGROUND

As literature and history are closely interconnected, it may be helpful to look for a moment at the historical conditions out of which our literature sprang.

Though conjecture has attempted to identify Iceland with the Ultima Thule of the ancients, the threads of authenticated history lead back only as far as the ninth century, when Iceland was, apparently, first discovered by the Norsemen. Naddod, an otherwise unknown Norse viking, is generally credited with priority in this discovery. It is supposed that he was accidentally driven upon the coast by storms while on his way from Norway to the Faroes, about 860. The second man said to have come to the island, whether by accident or design, was Gardar Svafarson, a Swede, who spent a winter there and named it Gardarsholm, after himself. About 865 a third man, Rafn-Floki, undertook the same voyage with the purpose of exploring the country, and evidently with the idea of possibly settling there, since he brought with him livestock. He called the country Iceland as the result of having seen a quantity of drift-ice in some of the firths on the north-western coast, and also, perhaps, because, through lack of foresight, he had suffered unnecessary hardship while wintering there.

These early voyagers carried back with them various and conflicting reports of the island. Their expeditions, while affording some knowledge of the country, might not have led to its colonization, had not other causes contributed to this effect. Within a short time Harald Fairhair, having been successful in subjugating the several small independent kingdoms of Norway, obtained sovereignty over the whole of the Norwegian realm, a victory finally marked by the battle of Hafsfirth in 872, according to Icelandic chronology. (The computation by which the historians arrived at this date cannot be traced; various scholars have shown a disposition to place it some twelve years later, i.e. *c.* 884.[1]) It is to this conquest that the Icelandic historians of the last period of the Commonwealth unanimously attribute the migration from Norway of which the settlement of Iceland and other colonies was the direct outcome. The change must inevitably have influenced the status of the other kings, the earls and great men, who, from independence and equality, power or voluntary allegiance, had to turn to face the unpleasant alternatives of either accepting the supreme authority of a ruler whom, in many cases, they regarded as having no more right to the sole kingship than themselves, or of fleeing the country before his avenging wrath. There has been much discussion as to how important a factor King Harald's so-called 'tyranny' was, but there seems little reason to doubt the substantial truth of this Icelandic tradition as to the causes of the Norwegian emigration. Considering the great number of prominent families and men who took part in it, it is likely that, in normal times, they would have had everything to lose and nothing to gain by leaving home.

Though King Harald's rise to supreme power may be regarded as the chief determinative of the general exodus from Norway, it would seem to have no bearing on the supposed earliest settlement, that of Ingolf Arnarson, explicitly stated in *Landnámabók* to have taken place in 874. Here again we are dealing with approximate and not absolute dating, as we do not know on what basis it was worked out. However this may be, Ingolf's leaving Norway, with Hjorleif, his foster-brother and brother-in-law, had no immediate connection with King Harald's success in gaining the supremacy, but was owing to their having incurred the enmity of Earl Atli the Lean of Gaular.

Thus it was that the settlement of Iceland from Norway began about 874 and continued for fifty or sixty years, the

[1] See H. Hermannsson's Introductory Essay, *Islandica*, Vol. xx, pp. 3–4, for discussion of the dating.

numbers being swelled a little by the addition of an element
of the same blood from less congenial and hospitable colonies
in the British Isles, and from Ireland in particular, where at
this time the Norwegian immigrants were being hard-pressed
by the native Celts. The families and dependents brought
to Iceland from these other communities introduced a foreign
strain, probably predominantly Celtic.

By 930 the period of land-taking was practically at an end,
and the abundance of space and unrestricted ground-tenure
which characterized the early years of the Settlement had
gradually given way to conditions in which closer contact
and greater restraint led to contention and rivalry. This time
of the migration was not conducive to intellectual activity
and creative effort. Even the Althing, introduced as the
central judicial legislative assembly of Iceland in 930, was
set up on the basis of laws modelled on the Norwegian, and,
in fact, actually obtained in their original form from that
country in 927–30.[1] Nor did the newly established Icelandic
Republic offer any immediate haven in which to pursue
literary or contemplative interests. The first seventy years
of its existence, with their struggles for district supremacy,
their fights in accordance with the demands of legalized
blood revenge, and their viking expeditions, were as nig-
gardly of leisure for the production of literature as they were
generous in supplying material for the compositions of a
later date.

Different conditions prevailed in Norway during the same
period. After Harald Fairhair had gained the supremacy,
such members of the royal and noble families as stayed in
the country grew gradually less turbulent, until by about
885 a peace was established which lasted, in the main un-
broken, for forty years. Toward the end of King Harald's
life, however, the vagueness of the laws of succession encouraged strife among his many sons. The reign of King

[1] 924 given as the date when Ulfljot went to Norway to draw up
laws with Gultingslov as a model. Finnur Jónsson, *Lit. Hist.*
Vol. I, p. 27.

Eric Blood-Axe[1] was ridden by unrest to such an extent that he was at last forced to surrender his authority to his younger half-brother, Hakon the Good,[2] and leave the country. After this conditions were again comparatively peaceful until trouble between Hakon and the sons of Eric marked the starting-point of another period of conflict and turmoil which lasted, more or less intermittently, throughout the eleventh and twelfth centuries. Though the respite from struggle was relatively short, King Harald Fairhair gave it great value through his fostering of Norwegian intellectual activity in general, and his support of, and regard for, skalds and their art[3] in particular. The seeds thus sown were destined to be carried to new fields of development in Iceland, while at the same time leaving uncut the links with Norway represented by Norwegian Eddic poems, and the tradition of entertainment by the telling of tales.

When Christianity was legally established in Iceland in 1000[4] the first unsettled period in the life of the colony may be said to have come to a close. After this date the country became more peaceful by degrees, as the protagonists of the earlier feuds left the stage, and, once established, comparatively quiet conditions within the country continued for about one hundred and fifty years.[5]

Between about 1025 and 1100 this tranquillity proved most favourable to the growth of oral tradition round the deeds of prowess and daring, of honour, loyalty and revenge, of the centuries preceding.[6] Nor was the stage geographically limited to Iceland and Norway. Expeditions in quest of distinction, advancement, adventure, power or riches, carried

---

[1] Son of King Harald Fairhair and Queen Ragnhild, daughter of King Eric of Jutland. According to Finnur Jónsson's edition of *Heimskringla* (by Snorri Sturluson), published 1911, p. 54.

[2] Son of King Harald Fairhair and Thora Mostrstöng, his high-born bond-maid. *Ibid.* p. 66.

[3] See definition of Skaldic poetry, pp. 2–3, above.

[4] See p. 3 above.

[5] Finnur Jónsson, *Lit. Hist.* Vol. II, p. 8.

[6] *Ibid.* p. 196.

Icelanders to Sweden and Denmark, to the British Isles, to the Faroes, the Orkneys, the Shetlands and the Hebrides, to the coasts of Normandy, and across Russia to the Court of Constantinople, where, with others of their race, they made up the Byzantine emperor's Varangian Guard. Many were in attendance on kings and earls as skalds, for, by the end of the tenth century, Icelanders were commonly thought of as the only Court poets[1] of the North, and the art of Skaldic poetry thus became, as it were, a national monopoly. From such travels men came back sooner or later to Iceland, bringing with them the stories of what they had done and seen and experienced in far distant lands. These accounts, as was the case with other information on past or present events, were spread throughout the country through the many and various contacts incident to gatherings of the people, first of all at the Althing and District-Things, but also at weddings, yule feasts, games and activities of like nature. A popular knowledge of history, fact and legend, based on transmission by word of mouth, was thus built up. It was out of this fund of material that the connected and organized Sagas on early times were welded together.

[1] See pp. 2–3 above for a definition of Skaldic or Court poetry. Norwegian Skalds fell silent with Eyvind Skalda-spillir, who died about 990; after him only a few men are mentioned as Skalds, and among these the Norwegian kings themselves. Finnur Jónsson, *Lit. Hist.* Vol. I, pp. 325–6, 449.

Chapter III

ADVERSITY AND PROSPERITY

IT is a striking feature of the dreams in Old Norse literature that they are predominantly concerned with adversity; many more relate to trouble than to good fortune. The majority of these deal with attack, with wounding at arms and violent death,[1] with treachery[2] and the burning of homesteads over the heads of their owners.[3] Only a few, proportionately, are connected with calamities owing either to the forces of nature[4] or to the worries and tragedies of everyday life[5] as distinct from those incident to strife and combat. Nevertheless, it is this smaller group which provides the measure of the field of adversity covered by the dreams. Spreading like a fan, they embrace a variety of subjects.

In representative collections of Icelandic folklore, dreams of adversity are also inclined to predominate, and many of the same type are to be found in allied folklores. Notwithstanding, there is a certain well-defined difference which distinguishes the folklore dreams from those of Old Norse literature. Whereas most of the adversity dreams in this literature have to do with the hostilities of men against men, those of folklore are primarily concerned with peril arising from the forces of nature,[6] from the activities of supernatural

[1] *Víga-Stýrs Saga ok Heiðarvíga*, p. 71; *Laxdæla Saga*, pp. 153–4; *Njáls Saga*, pp. 326–7; *Sturlunga Saga*, Vol. I, p. 494; *Hrómundar Saga Greipssonar*, *Fas.* II, pp. 335–6.

[2] *Vatnsdæla Saga*, p. 90; *þorsteins Saga Síðu-Hallssonar*, pp. 24–6.

[3] *Hænsa-þóris Saga*, p. 18.

[4] *Laxdæla Saga*, pp. 89, 226.

[5] *Gunnlaugs Saga Ormstungu*, pp. 3–4; *Víga-Glúms Saga*, pp. 25–6; *þáttr Ólafs Geirstaða Álfs*, *Fms.* 10, pp. 210–11; *Jómsvíkinga Saga*, *Fms.* 11, pp. 5–6.

[6] Jón Árnason, *þjóðsögur og Æfintýri*, Vol. II, *Draugasögur*, pp. 10, 11; Sigfús Sigfússon, *Íslenzkar þjóðsögur og Sagnir*, Vol. II, pp. 13, 14.

beings,[1] from the visitations of the dead,[2] or from the general calamities of epidemic[3] or famine.[4]

So strong is the element of human aggression in the adversity dreams of Old Norse literature that it is not altogether surprising to find that, among the dreams of prosperity, there are more which relate to successful attacks on the dreamer's enemies,[5] or to help in such ventures, than to any other one thing; in this category are included dreams dealing with advice and information contributing directly to the chances of victory in a battle,[6] or with the acquiring of weapons by means of which fights against odds may be won.[7] The degree to which considerations of strife obtrude themselves in the dreams is not, however, as great in the prosperity as in the adversity group. Matters foreign to the fortunes of conflict thus have more relative importance here. Gifts of proficiency in the art of poetry,[8] gifts of gold or of objects endowed with magic powers of healing,[9] stand side by side with gifts of weapons. We also find dreams relating to the birth of children, to the distinguished character of future descendants,[10] to the contracting of happy marriages[11] or the terminating of unhappy ones,[12] to the coming of

[1] Jón Þorkelsson, *Þjóðsögur og Munnmæli*, Vol. I, pp. 28, 29, 184; Sigurður Nordal and Þórbergur Þórðarson, *Gráskinna*, 1928, p. 8.

[2] Jón Árnason, *Þjóðsögur og Æfintýri*, Vol. II, *Draugasögur*, pp. 15, 26; Jón Þorkelsson, *Þjóðsögur og Munnmæli*, Vol. I, p. 32.

[3] Sigfús Sigfússon, *Íslenzkar Þjóðsögur og Sagnir*, Vol. II, pp. 36–7, 38–9.

[4] *Ibid.* p. 31.

[5] Magnus Olsen, *Sturlunga Saga*, Vol. I, p. 432 and Vol. II, p. 232; *Sverris Saga*, Fms. 8, pp. 106–8.

[6] *Þorsteins Saga Síðu-Hallssonar*, p. 20.

[7] *Flóamanna Saga*, p. 26.

[8] *Þórleifs Þáttr Jarlsskálds*, Fjörutíu Íslendinga Þættir, pp. 397–8.

[9] *Þórsteins Þáttr Uxafóts*, Fjörutíu Íslendinga Þættir, pp. 448–51; *Flóamanna Saga*, p. 27; *Þorskfirðinga Saga*, pp. 8–9.

[10] *Heimskringla*, p. 39; *Flóamanna Saga*, p. 46.

[11] *Flóamanna Saga*, p. 45; Magnus Olsen, *Völsunga Saga*, p. 61.

[12] *Laxdæla Saga*, p. 88.

prosperous times,[1] to personal success,[2] or happiness after death.[3]

The dreams of prosperity in folklore are, in some measure, expressed through the same channels as those of adversity. Both the dead and the supposed supernatural entities have their friendly as well as their hostile aspects;[4] they can serve, as well as wound or destroy man. Treasure[5] is also counted among the prosperity dreams of folklore, while the question of marriage[6] is more in evidence here than in the dreams of adversity. It is important to notice that the dream relating to success in personal hostility, so conspicuous in the Sagas, disappears almost entirely in folklore.

These are some of the outstanding characteristics which distinguish the adversity and prosperity dreams of Old Norse literature and folklore respectively, and, although certain differences between the two groups have been brought to light, these serve largely to show the dimensions of the field jointly covered by them. For, if the adversity dreams of Old Norse literature provide warrant for the dreams concerned with the grim perils inherent in the forces of nature,[7] those of folklore include examples dealing with personal hostility;[8] if the prosperity dreams of Old Norse literature embody specimens of the dream in which supernatural beings figure,[9] those of folklore preserve, in a few instances, examples relating to success in personal hostility.[10] It seems clear that,

[1] *Flóamanna Saga,* p. 46.
[2] Ari Þorgilsson's *Íslendingabók,* p. 8; *Flóamanna Saga,* p. 45.
[3] *Gísla Saga Súrssonar,* p. 73; *Flóamanna Saga,* p. 42.
[4] Jón Þorkelsson, *Þjóðsögur og Munnmæli,* Vol. I, p. 345; Sigfús Sigfússon, *Íslenzkar Þjóðsögur og Sagnir,* Vol. II, p. 29.
[5] Jón Árnason, *Þjóðsögur og Æfintýri,* Vol. III, *Uppvakningar og Fylgjur,* pp. 67–8.
[6] Jón Árnason, *Þjóðsögur og Æfintýri,* Vol. III, *Galdrasögur,* pp. 245, 246; Oddur Björnsson and Jónas Rafnar, *Gríma,* No. I, pp. 36, 37.
[7] *Laxdæla Saga,* pp. 89, 226.
[8] Sigfús Sigfússon, *Íslenzkar Þjóðsögur og Sagnir,* Vol. I, p. 83.
[9] *Laxdæla Saga,* p. 161; *Landnámabók, Hauksbók,* p. 101; *Gísla Saga Súrssonar,* p. 73.
[10] Jón Árnason, *Þjóðsögur og Æfintýri,* Vol. I, *Útilegumannasögur,* p. 9.

while the relative prominence of adversity and prosperity types of dream remains substantially unchanged in Old Norse literature and folklore, the subjects with which they deal show a change of emphasis and balance when the one is weighed against the other, rather than sharp divergences and startling innovations. Nevertheless, the matter of the dreams in Old Norse literature and folklore, in spite of many inter-connections, is not, apparently, coextensive. There are some dreams in Old Norse literature with which I have not been able to find affinities in folklore.[1]

The divisions of adversity and prosperity are the most inclusive into which the dreams fall, and, indeed, could we but always know the effect on the mind of the dreamer, would no doubt cover them all, either as pure or combined[2] types. As long as the dreamer himself derived any form of pleasure or displeasure from a dream we may surely place it under this designation. But, as has been intimated, it is sometimes virtually impossible to consign a given dream definitely to one or the other category, or to a combination of the two; we cannot always tell how directions or exhortations contained in a dream appeal to the dreamer, and sometimes the dream seems to concern the interests of a dream agent[3] rather than those of the dreamer.[4] In such cases as do not lend themselves to assignment to one or both of these divisions, it will, of course, be necessary to leave the individual dream out of account here, but this is by no means tantamount to suggesting that they do not belong in this classification; it merely shows that our knowledge of these particular dreams is insufficient to determine their position within it. The universality of these groups must be admitted unless we dare to postulate the possibility of dreams

[1] *Víga-Glúms Saga*, p. 59; Magnus Olsen, *Sturlunga Saga*, Vol. 1, pp. 258–9.
[2] *Laxdæla Saga*, p. 90.
[3] Being appearing in a dream for a specific purpose, such as commanding that a thing be done, etc.
[4] *Fóstbræðra Saga*, p. 115.

relating to matters of complete indifference to the dreamer, and this seems unthinkable in an absolute form. Such dreams would neither fulfil the requirements, nor conform to the nature, of tradition, as I see it, and, in addition, would be psychologically unsound. It is not the unimportant and unremarkable events and activities which we expect to find carried down by tradition, nor would anything so untrue to psychology as a dream entirely dissociated from the wishes and fears of the dreamer stand the test of time.

The environmental reasons for the differences between the adversity and prosperity dreams in question are almost too obvious to call for discussion. Suffice it to say that the life of tenth-century Iceland, enlightened and well organized as conditions were for the time, was very different from that of the end of the nineteenth or the beginning of the twentieth century; however far back folklore runs, it comes down to modern days. In the Saga Age, as we have seen, the more striking and noteworthy dangers were bound up with the rigorously regulated system of blood revenge through the balance of which the country was, in large measure, governed. In later times, with responsible and centralized government taking the place of the more or less individualistic law expedients of pioneer days, it is the sea, the blizzard, the mysterious forces of the earth, and the dead which bulk large. The meaning of prosperity also gives evidence of having changed in folklore. On the one hand, there seems to be more of a withdrawal from the realities of life, and on the other, at least in one direction, a greater insistence on the material. Treasure in the form of actual money, or of gold and silver, is met with in Icelandic folklore much more frequently than in Old Norse literature, and a certain emphasis on this theme, in such Danish folklore dreams as I have collected, suggests that this variation of the treasure *motif* may have come to Iceland from that wealthier country. It is natural, too, in different times, that the same type of dream should come to apply to different things. A magic weapon given to a dreamer, in the Sagas, to help him overcome an enemy is, in folklore[1], matched by a magic scythe with which to reap grain. A Saga dream containing advice as to how to win a battle[2] is comparable with a folklore dream showing how lost sheep, stolen by outlaws, may be recovered by force.[3] The temper of the dreams with which we are dealing is, from this point of view, a reflection of the life out of which it sprang, of which it is one expression, and of which it is itself a part.

[1] Jón Árnason, *Þjóðsögur og Æfintýri*, Vol. I, *Huldufólkssögur*, p. 8.
[2] *Knytlínga Saga, Fms.* 11, p. 371.
[3] Jón Árnason, *Þjóðsögur og Æfintýri*, Vol. I, *Útilegumannasögur*, p. 9.

Chapter IV

SYMBOLIC IMAGES IN DREAMS

FETCHES, GUARDIAN SPIRITS, TROLLS AND GODS

IF none of the dreams are matters of complete indifference, it is clear that the individual dream has in itself its own value and significance. From the standpoint of tradition, one of the most interesting and important aspects of particular dreams is that of the imagery they contain. In examining this question we shall begin with such symbolic images as, at once, relate primarily to pre-Christian thought, partake of the heathen conceptions of the unknown and the mysterious, and are yet closely bound up with human beings.

FETCHES

People who figure in the dreams of Old Norse literature often appear in a fetch guise. The fetch is the inherent soul, the accompanying counterpart or representation, of a living person. Usually invisible, it may, nevertheless, be seen in dreams and visions, almost always in the form of an animal. The possession of a fetch is universal, and its character coincides, in some salient feature or features, with the qualities and characteristics of the person to whom it belongs, or, especially in cases of hostility, with the attitude of its owner toward the dreamer.

As the extent to which fetches are found in the dreams is considerable, so also the forms they take, and the dream situations in which they play a part, are alike various.

It is interesting to note, in the first place, that a given person is not invariably portrayed by the same fetch, even in dreams of similar content and significance. In the dreams of King Atli prophetic of the slaying of his two sons, the boys are represented, in one instance, as hawks flying from his arm to the domain of the dead,[1] in another as whelps, torn from him, and turning to corpses before him.[2] Again, in the dreams of Kostbera, wife of Högni, foretelling the treachery of King Atli against her husband and his brother Gunnarr, the hostile king appears, once as a bear breaking up the high-seat of the hall,[3] and next as an eagle flying through the room and sprinkling everyone with blood.[4] In *Gísla Saga Súrssonar* the slayer of Vésteinn is depicted as a viper[5] and a wolf[6] in Gísli's two dreams of foreboding, respectively.

But if the animal attached to a person as his fetch is not always the same, there seems to be a certain likeness between the animals with which a person may be identified. The hawks on King Atli's arm, and the whelps which are torn from him, by their own nature and condition, call forth something akin to the care of the father for his sons, and themselves typify some phases of filial dependence. If King Atli appears in successive dreams as a bear and an eagle, each of these has the attributes of great strength, courage and distinction, qualities well suited to a mighty ruler. The viper and the wolf in Gísli's dreams are both dangerous and of evil connotation. The fetches by which an individual may be depicted are thus related to each other, in that they have outstanding characteristics in common, such being those which distinguish the person.

A fetch, by appropriate appearance and activity, may also express its owner's attitude of the moment, or his specific intention, if it does not actually mirror his deeds at the time of their performance. The bear fetch of King Atli breaks

---

[1] *Guþrúnarkviða*, II (en forna), *Die Lieder der Edda* (ed. B. Sijmons), p. 406, verse 42; Magnus Olsen, *Völsunga Saga*, p. 90.

[2] *Guþrúnarkviða*, II (en forna), *Die Lieder der Edda* (ed. B. Sijmons), p. 406, verse 43; Magnus Olsen, *Völsunga Saga*, p. 90.

[3] *Atlamöl en grønlenzko*, *Die Lieder der Edda* (ed. B. Sijmons), p. 441, verse 16; Magnus Olsen, *Völsunga Saga*, p. 93.

[4] *Atlamöl en grønlenzko*, *Die Lieder der Edda* (ed. B. Sijmons), p. 441, verse 18; Magnus Olsen, *Völsunga Saga*, pp. 93, 94.

[5] *Gísla Saga Súrssonar*, p. 29.   [6] *Ibid.*

up the high-seat, shakes his paws terrifyingly, and takes everyone into his mouth at once, thus showing his attitude and intention toward Högni and Gunnarr. When Gunnarr of Hlíðarendi, with two companions, goes, on behalf of his kinswoman, Unnr, to trick her divorced husband, Hrútr, into hearing a legal court summons, Höskuldr, half-brother of Hrútr, has a dream: He sees a great bear, followed by two cubs, making for Hrútr's homestead.[1] This dream occurs, as nearly as we can tell from the Saga, either at the time of Gunnarr's arrival at Hrútr's homestead or shortly afterward. Alternately, the fetch may indicate attitudes and intentions, or carry out activities which are to arise or come to pass in the future. In *Vápnfirðinga Saga*[2] a dream told by Brodd-Helgi's foster-mother outlines, through the symbolism of ox fetches, all the main factors in the further course of the Saga.

Of such weight is attitude and purpose in fetch representation, indeed, that the wolf is a common and recognized form for a person or persons making an attack at arms. Wolves, howling at both ends of a sword stuck through Gunnarr, figure in a dream of Glaumvör, his wife, indicative of King Atli's hostility toward him.[3] Before the onslaught of Barði Guðmundarson on the Borgfirthers, Gísli Þorgautsson, one among them, has a dream of warning in which wolves rush upon himself and his brothers, and deal roughly with them, as they are reaping in the meadow.[4] The leader of an expedition, however, is, even here, often marked out from his followers by a special fetch; in the dream of Þórbjörg, prophetic of her brother's hostilities against his unsympathetic brother-in-law, Hörðr appears as a white bear, while the members of his band are depicted as wolves.[5] When Þorgrímr Dýrason, a man versed in wizardry and spells, is on his way

[1] *Njáls Saga*, ch. 23, p. 54.   [2] Ch. 16, pp. 25, 26.
[3] *Átlamöl en grønlenzko, Die Lieder der Edda* (ed. B. Sijmons), p. 442, verse 22; Magnus Olsen, *Völsunga Saga*, p. 94.
[4] *Víga-Styrs Saga ok Heiðarvíga*, p. 71.
[5] *Harðar Saga ok Hólmverja*, p. 66.

with a company of men to attack Hávarðr Ísfirðingr in connection with a blood feud, Atli of Otradalr, Hávarðr's host and protector, dreams of the expedition as a pack of eighteen wolves led by a vixen.[1]

The foregoing examples comprise a fair selection of the animals which play the part of fetches in the Elder Edda and the historical Sagas. One more dream, however, seems worthy of particular attention from this point of view. The horse is so closely associated with the gods that it is hard to think of it as representing a human being under any circumstances. The Prose Edda furnishes a list of the names of the horses of the Æsir.[2] Sleipnir, Óðinn's eight-legged steed, is itself almost a divinity,[3] and in *Hrafnkels Saga Freysgoða*[4] there is a record of a horse dedicated to the god Freyr. Nevertheless, in *Vatnsdæla Saga*,[5] we find a dream which seems to show a connection between the horse and the fetch.

Vatnsdalr is without a chief after the death of Ingólfr Þorsteinsson, and, in accordance with custom, a meeting is called to elect a man to hold the chieftainship and look after affairs until the heirs, still minor, shall come of age. A certain man named Þorkell Silfri, a shape-changer,[6] clever, powerful and wealthy, but unpopular and with few friends, hopes to be chosen. His wife tries to prevent him from attending the meeting, saying that he is not fitted to be chief in Vatnsdalr, but he insists. The night before the assembly is to be held he has a dream and tells it to Signý, his wife:[7]

[1] *Hávarðar Saga Ísfirðings*, p. 59.
[2] *Gylfaginning*, ch. 15.   [3] *Ibid.* ch. 42.
[4] *Hrafnkels Saga Freysgoða*, pp. 4 ff.   [5] *Vatnsdæla Saga*, p. 104.
[6] Sorcerer, capable of changing his shape at will.
[7] *Vatnsdæla Saga*, ch. 42, pp. 104 ff.: 'Þorkel silfra dreymdi ena næstu nótt áðr fundrinn var, ok sagði Signýju konu sinni, at hann þóttist ríða ofan eftir Vatnsdal hesti rauðum, ok þótti honum trautt við jörðina koma—"ok vil ek svá ráða, at rautt mun fyrir brenna ok til virðingar snúa". Signý kvaðst annan veg ætla—"sýnist mér þetta illr draumr". ok kvað hest mar heita, enn mar er mannsfylgja, ok kvað rauða sýnast ef blóðug yrði—"ok má vera, at þú sér veginn á fundinum, ef þú ætlar þér goðorðit, því at nógir munu þér þess fyrirmuna"'.

'He dreamed that he was riding down along Vatnsdalr on a red horse; it seemed to him that the horse scarcely touched the ground'. Þorkell interprets this to mean that 'as red is for bright prospects, so matters will turn out to my honour'. But Signý thinks it otherwise, and says it is an evil dream. She tells him that a horse is called a *marr*, and that *marr* means a man's fetch and that it (the fetch) looks red when it is bloody—'and it may be that you will be slain at the meeting if you think of obtaining the chieftainship, for many will grudge it you'.

Signý's interpretation proves to be right. Þorkell, after having been chosen as chief by the drawing of lots, is slain at the meeting by the boy, Þorkell Krafla, at the instigation of his father, Þorgrímr Hallormsson, who, as a kinsman of the former chief, has a strong motive for preventing the chieftainship from falling into unsuitable and unworthy hands.

If it were not that the extant version of *Vatnsdæla Saga* is late, it is quite possible that we should not have had this instance of a horse interpreted as a fetch. Finnur Jónsson[1] estimates that, while the original Saga, used in *Landnáma-bók's* oldest form,[2] was probably no later than about 1200, the present poorer version cannot date before approximately 1300. He speaks of various minor mistakes and inaccuracies which suggest revision and interpolation, and comments upon the post-classical character of the language. In dealing with late words he points out, among other examples, that the expression *mar er mannsfylgja* is an impossible linguistic collocation which depends on the confounding of the words *marr* and *mara*.[3] If, then, the present Saga is a product of

---

[1] *Den Oldnorske og Oldislandske Litteraturs Historie*, Vol. II, pp. 476–7.
[2] *Landnámabók, Melabók*, p. 249.
[3] G. Vigfússon, *Icelandic-English Dictionary*, pp. 412–13: '*Marr* means steed, and *mara* means nightmare conceived as ogress'. Compare the nightmare (?) of King Vanlandi Sveigðisson in which a mare (*mara*) treads him to death in his sleep. *Heimskringla, Ynglinga Saga*, ch. 13, pp. 11–12.

the end of the thirteenth or the beginning of the fourteenth century, it is to be expected that tradition should be distorted, and old conceptions dimmed. With the passing of three hundred years since the introduction of Christianity, it may surely be that the inappropriateness of a horse as the representative of a man was no longer insistently apparent. What could never have been tolerated while the old religion was remembered as a vital faith could stand after time and Christianity had robbed it of its life and colour. The heathen gods were, to some degree, forgotten, and the horse used as a fetch in the same way as any other animal. Moreover, if we look at the chapter in which it is found, it seems more than likely that this dream is a straight interpolation, since it figures in the second of two versions of the conversation between Þorkell Silfri and his wife before he goes to the meeting, these being within half a page of each other.[1] I hazard these suggestions for what they may be worth.

But the fetch is not quite always in the form of an animal.[2] In *Bjarnar Saga Hítdælakappa*,[3] Björn Arngeirsson has a dream in which men are represented by fetches which are evidently replicas of their owners. This is the only dream I have come across in Old Norse literature, the human figures in which are specifically described as 'fetches of men'; it is, perhaps, the more remarkable in that, as a dream of armed attack, it might normally have been expected to make use of the wolf fetch. Nor can it be argued that this unusual fetch form is manifestly the outcome of post-classical influence. Finnur Jónsson places this Saga as not later than before 1250, and considers it as still within the bounds of the classical group.[4] There is evidence, though, of kinship between this fetch type and one which figures in a dream from an earlier Saga. *Gísla Saga Súrssonar*, the first

[1] *Vatnsdæla Saga*, pp. 103, 104.
[2] See definition of Fetch, p. 17, above; I. Reichborn-Kjennerud, *Vår Gamle Trolldomsmedisin*, p. 38.
[3] *Bjarnar Saga Hítdælakappa*, ch. 25, p. 59.
[4] Finnur Jónsson, *Lit. Hist.* Vol. II, p. 420.

version of which dates from about 1200,[1] contains a dream of Gísli in which the leader of an attacking band appears as a man with the head of a wolf.[2] Whether the men who follow him are to be understood as fetches in human shape there seems to be no way of definitely discovering. However, it is interesting to note that, whereas, in the first dream, we are given no sign that the human fetches are more determinative of identity than animal ones, in the second the dreamer recognizes Eyjólfr Þórðarson, the man who, though he does not lead in the actual attack on Gísli, is really in command of the expedition.[3] This fact rather suggests, to my mind, that the *Bjarnar Saga* dream shows more of the true characteristics of the fetch, which is identified, not by personal recognition, but by equation of its qualities with those of the individual to whom it belongs. On the other hand, as may be seen from the dream in question, the evidence for this argument is purely negative, and, in the case of Gísli's dream, it is hard to conceive of real men and the fetch of a man being placed, indiscriminately, side by side.

The fetches found in the dreams of the legendary Sagas are somewhat different.[4] Other animals, some fabulous and some foreign, make their appearance, and even such as we are accustomed to from the historical Sagas may assume a brilliance and splendour consistent with retreat from the stern requirements of reality. Thus, Guðrún Gjúkadóttir dreams of her future husband, Sigurðr Sigmundarson Fafnísbani, as a hawk whose feathers are the colour of gold.[5] Among beasts which we have not met with before are swine,

---

[1] Finnur Jónsson, *Lit. Hist.* Vol. ii, pp. 453, 458.

[2] *Gísla Saga Súrssonar*, pp. 81–2.

[3] *Ibid.* pp. 85, 86. The man detailed by Eyjólfr to lead in the encounter, and who is represented as a man with a wolf's head, is Njósnar-Helgi.

[4] This is not intended to include those dreams in the *Fornaldarsögur* which are also contained in the Elder Edda.

[5] Magnus Olsen, *Völsunga Saga*, p. 61. See dream in *Gunnlaug Saga Ormstungu*, pp. 3–4.

boar, stag,[1] leopard, lion, and, of imaginary creatures, the dragon.

The hostile force of King Óláfr of Garðar is represented in one of the dreams told to King Haddingr by Blindr hinn Illi (which, however, do not, apparently, belong to the original Saga) as a herd of swine, rooting up the ground with their snouts.[2] In *Sögubrot af Fornkonungum*,[3] a fragment relating to Denmark,[4] we find a prophetic dream in which stag, leopard and winged dragon stand side by side with the more familiar bear. In this, the dreamer, King Hrœrekr, is himself the stag, his brother, King Helgi, is the leopard, the wicked King Ívarr is the winged dragon, and King Hrœrekr's wife and their son are the bear and bear cub. Perhaps as a token of the distinction and nobility of King Helgi, victim of his brother's hand through the base misrepresentations of King Ívarr, the leopard is described as having a mane like gold. Queen Ingigerðr, in her dream announcing the second attempt of King Hrólfr Gautreksson to claim the hand of her daughter, sees the expedition as many wolves led by a lion accompanied and supported by two white bears and a savage boar.[5]

As products of the more or less free imagination fostered by the medium of legend, these dreams show a tendency toward excess of differentiation and contrast, an exaggeration and over-emphasis on the external and the descriptive, which, in itself, enhances the impression of unreality and wonder. While some of the fetch forms in the *Fornaldarsögur* are thus distinctive and largely peculiar to themselves, they are by no means exclusive of those which figure in Sagas not invested with the glamour of the prehistoric past.[6]

[1] But see possible play on the name Hjörtr (stag) in Gunnarr's dream. *Njáls Saga*, pp. 144–5.
[2] *Hrómundar Saga Greipssonar, Fas.* II, p. 335.
[3] *Sögubrot af Fornkonungum, Fas.* I, p. 288.
[4] Probably founded on *Skjöldunga Saga*. Finnur Jónsson, *Lit. Hist.* Vol. II, p. 829.
[5] *Hrólfs Saga Gautrekssonar, Fas.* III, p. 70.
[6] *Hervarar Saga ok Heiðreks, Fas.* I, p. 313.

Various conceptions of the nature of the fetch proper are exemplified in connection with dreams. That it was sometimes thought of as a form of the person himself is clear from the words of Kostbera about the eagle of her dream: 'I thought it was the shape of Atli'.[1] The idea that the fetch is the soul or ego of its owner which leaves the body during sleep is implied when Þorgrímr Dýrason,[2] on waking, says: 'I have been at the stead awhile, but it is so bewildering to me, that I do not know how it will turn out'.[3] From the attacking wolf fetch, which, under appropriate circumstances, may supersede a person's normal fetch, we are already acquainted with the fetch conceived as attitude.[4] From this point of view it is called *hugr*, i.e. will or intention, mind. When Atli speaks of his dream of hostile wolves, he declares: 'I know for a certainty that these are the *hugir* of men'.[5] Eiðr, in interpreting the attacking wolf dream of his foster-father, says: 'It is evident that this means that there are evil wills of men against you'.[6] In Þorsteinn's interpretation of his own dream prophetic of the coming of enemies, he refers to wolf fetches as an expression of *vargahug* (wolfish wills or intentions).[7] In its protective character the fetch appears as a companion and supporter of its owner: 'These are the fetches of your enemies: the ox accompanies (supports, belongs to) Þorvarðr, and the bull Hallr', says the foster-mother of Eyjólfr Guðmundarson in interpreting his dream foretelling strife at the Thing.[8] These conceptions as to the intrinsic character of the fetch, as such, are closely interrelated as different aspects of personality or 'soul'.[9]

[1] *Atlamöl en grønlenʒko, Die Lieder der Edda* (ed. B. Sijmons), p. 441, verse 18; Magnus Olsen, *Völsunga Saga*, pp. 93, 94.
[2] Þorgrímr Dýrason is on an expedition to attack the homestead of Atli of Otradalr.
[3] *Hávarðar Saga Ísfirðings*, p. 60.   [4] See p. 19 above.
[5] *Hávarðar Saga Ísfirðings*, p. 59.
[6] *þórðar Saga Hrædu*, p. 19.
[7] *þorsteins Saga Víkingssonar, Fas.* II, p. 77.
[8] *Ljósvetninga Saga*, pp. 96–7.
[9] Compare I. Reichborn-Kjennerud, *Vår Gamle Trolldomsmedisin*, pp. 37–9.

Fetches figure rather sparingly in the dreams of folklore. From Iceland we have the story of a father who has a son and daughter, twins. These two go on a moss-gathering expedition. The night before they go the father dreams that he has two white birds which he thinks a great deal of. He loses the hen bird and misses her much. He interprets this rightly to mean that he will soon lose his daughter, and is much troubled. She is stolen by outlaws while away.[1] It is obvious that this has much in common with King Atli's hawk dream,[2] and it bears a strong likeness to the dream of King Gormr in which the two sons he is to have appear as white birds.[3] Another echo from the Elder Edda is found in the dream of Adelud, prophetic of the slaying of her husband through jealousy.[4] A white bear rushes upon the husband and strikes him with his heavy paw.[5] Palli, in a Danish source,[6] dreams of two falcons and two bears; they try to tear him to pieces. He tells his wife and she knows what it means. He has betrayed her father and two brothers. She still has two brothers left, however, and they are to take revenge by slaying Palli. From Sweden we have an example in which the behaviour and number of King Swerker's own falcons, seen by his daughter in a dream, announce his death, and in which a fight between an eagle and a vulture (*gam*) represents the struggle between the father, King Swerker, and the lover.[7] This fight between eagle and vulture may be compared with the dream in *Gunnlaugs Saga Ormstungu*, in which two great eagles come to death grips over Helga en fagra.[8] The viper or snake fetch figures both as an evil or hostile person, as in *Gisla*

[1] Jón Árnason, *þjóðsögur og Æfintýri*, Vol. I, *Útilegumannasögur*, p. 41.
[2] See pp. 17–18 above.   [3] Saxo Grammaticus, Book IX, pp. 387–8.
[4] See p. 18 above, Kostbera's dream of King Atli.
[5] Svend Grundtvig and Jón Sigurðsson, *Íslenzk Fornkvæði*, I, No. 28.
[6] *Danmarks Gamle Folkeviser*, No. 324.
[7] Aug. Afzelius, *Svenska Folkets Sago-Häfder*, Vol. IV, p. 15.
[8] *Gunnlaugs Saga Ormstungu*, ch. 2, pp. 3–4.

Saga Súrssonar,[1] and as a descendant, as in *Biskupa Sögur.*[2] In a dream from the same Swedish source as above,[3] the future achievements of two small boys are seen by their grandmother in the climbing of two snakes up the church wall. The one who is to be the most distinguished crawls to the top of the steeple, the other tumbles to the ground when only half-way up. In Danish folklore, there is a saying that 'when vipers pursue us in dreams, they are wicked people who wish to do us harm'.[4] Norwegian folklore gives us what may be a reflection of the converse of this: 'To dream of snakes always means something good'.[5] A dragon from a Danish story, standing for a plurality of robbers, or their intention, is the only affinity I have found with the dragon fetch of the *Fornaldarsögur.*[6] Here, both parents of three little brothers dream one night 'that a hideous dragon has dragged them to its lair in the forest'.[7] The same summer, as the boys are playing outside one day, they are carried off by robbers. Another *Fornaldarsögur* type of fetch, the lion,[8] figures in a dream from a West Highland folktale. The young King of Lochlann has sent four of his best warriors to cut off the head of Conall, son of the King of Eirinn. Conall has a dream of warning[9]:

It seemed to him that he was going on a road that went through the midst of a gloomy wood, and it seemed to him that

[1] *Gisla Saga Súrssonar*, p. 29.
[2] *Sögubrot um Jón Árnason, Bks.* II, pp. 421–2.
[3] Aug. Afzelius, *Svenska Folkets Sago-Häfder*, Vol. IV, p. 38.
[4] E. T. Kristensen, *Jydske Folkeminder*, Vol. VI, p. 283: 'Naar hugorme vil komme efter os i drømme, er det onde mennesker der vil gjøre os fortræd'.
[5] *Folkevennen*, No. 95, p. 383: 'At drømme om orme betyder altid noget godt'.
[6] See p. 24 above, footnotes 2 and 3.
[7] E. T. Kristensen, *Danske Sagn, som de har lydt i folkemunde*, Vol. IV, p. 404: 'En nat drømte begge forældrene at en hæslig drage havde slæbt dem til sin hule inde i skoven'.
[8] *Hrólfs Saga Gautrekssonar, Fas.* III, pp. 56–7, 70.
[9] J. F. Campbell, *Popular Tales of the West Highlands*, Vol. III, pp. 224–5.

he saw four lions before him, two on the upper side of the road, and two on the lower side, and they were gnashing their teeth, and switching their tails, making ready to spring upon him, and it seemed to him that it was easier for the lions that were on the upper side of the road to leap down, than it was for the lions that were on the lower side to leap up; and it was better for him to slay those that were on the upper side first, and he gave a cheery spring to be at them; and he sprang aloft through his sleep, and he struck his head against a tie beam (*sail shuimear*) that was across above him in the house of the 'Tamhasgan', and he drove as much as the breadth of a half-crown piece of the skin off the top of his head, and then he was aroused, and he said to Duanach,—

'I myself was dreaming, Duanach', and he told him his dream.

And Duanach said, 'Thy dream is a dainty to read. Go thou out to the stone of the Tamhasg, and thou wilt see the four best warriors that the King of Lochlann has, two on each side of the stone round about it, sharpening their swords to take off thy head'.

Conall went out with his blade in his hand, and he took off their heads, and he left two heads on each side of the stone of the Tamhasg,....

A possible connection with the problematical horse fetch of *Vatnsdæla Saga*[1] is found in Danish folklore: Helli Hagen's mother dreams that the good foal her son is to ride stumbles. Helli gets into a fight and is slain.[2] A possible variation of the human form of fetch is found in a dream (Icelandic) in which six human heads, falling from a boat into the sea, stand for six men who are to be lost in shipwreck.[3]

The above are fetches in folklore which have counter-

---

[1] See pp. 20–2 above.

[2] Svend Grundtvig, *Danmarks Gamle Folkeviser*, Vols. I–VIII, p. 47 f., No. 5, verse 3: 'Grimilds Hævn. Dett vor Helli Hagens moder, hun drømpte saa underlig: At den gode foole styrte som hand skulle hen riide'.

[3] Sigurður Nordal and Þórbergur Þórðarson, *Gráskinna*, 1928, p. 5.

parts in Old Norse literature. Some are exactly like those of Edda and Saga, while others have, to a certain extent, changed. The dragon, prophetic of the stealing of the three little boys, represents, not one person or individual attitude as in Old Norse literature, but several persons or their collective wills. Also, the falcons of King Swerker, announcing his death by their pitiful behaviour, seem to suggest that, as his possessions, they are bound to him by a spiritual tie, which, in a sense, identifies them with himself. Another dream in which the same idea occurs is that of Benedikt Knudson, indicating the death of his betrothed.[1] He sees his two falcons, turned grey, with their wings swathed in silk, lying at his feet. (It may, perhaps, even be hazarded that the idea has, in this instance, gone a step further; for, in the same way, his red cloak has turned black, and its ermine lining has been stolen away. That is, inanimate objects seem here to take on and express the mental and emotional state of the dreamer.) As for the viper, it has become a fixed symbol in Danish folklore, and is permanently associated with evil people, while in Norway the meaning of snake dreams is equally established, though the connection with the fetch is not specific.

It is interesting to note that seals make their appearance as fetches in Icelandic folklore. Snæbjörn dreams of six seals which are lost in spite of his efforts to save them; they stand for six men who are to be victims of a shipwreck.[2] In Scottish folklore we find that 'to dream of being bitten by dogs or cats is interpreted as the plotting of enemies';[3] in Danish folklore, to dream of being bitten by dogs or

[1] Svend Grundtvig, *Danmarks Gamle Folkeviser*, Vols. I–VIII, Copenhagen, 1853–1904, No. 455, verses 3, 4: 'Mig drømthe, min røde skarlagenn var bleffuen sort det hermelin, der under sadt, och det var stollenn bort. Mig drømthe, det minne falcke tho dy var bleffuen graa, derris vinger var suøbt y silcke, di for min foder laa'.

[2] Sigurður Nordal and Þórbergur Þórðarson, *Gráskinna*, 1928, pp. 10, 11.

[3] Walter Gregor, *Notes on the Folklore of the North-East of Scotland*, p. 29.

gored by bulls means that one is the victim of gossip;[1] this
suggests, to my mind, a reflection of the fetch idea. Various
folklores depict the soul as a small animal, often seen leaving
the body of its associate.[2] This conception, although at first
sight it seems like that of our Northern fetch, is not really
related to it. Whereas the former survives the death of its
owner, the life of the latter is dependent upon that of the
person whose fetch it is. 'Its death is the portent of the
death of its owner, and this not only when its death is seen
in dreams.'[3] A variant form of the soul objectively seen
by a waking observer is found in Icelandic folklore; here
it appears as a puff of smoke.[4] In spite of the few examples
which bear witness to its survival, the heathen fetch tends
to disappear in the dreams of folklore, to be replaced
by a soul form which has the Christian attribute of immortality.

GUARDIAN SPIRITS

The *hamingja* is the guardian spirit of the family, and is
primarily attached to its head. This tutelary genius is in the
form of a woman, but beings of the same character and performing kindred functions are the *dísir* or *spákonur* (sometimes identified with the valkyries),[5] and the *spámaðr*, while
an antithesis to these is represented by the evil genius. On
the death of the person to whom it is attached, the guardian
spirit[6] passes to that member of the family chosen as his

[1] Svend Grundtvig, *Gamle Danske Minder*, No. 2, pp. 245 ff.
[2] O. Grønborg, *Optegnelser paa Vendelbomaal*, Copenhagen, 1884,
pp. 144 ff.
[3] Hastings' *Encyclopædia of Religion and Ethics*, Vol. xi, B. S.
Phillpotts, 'Soul (Teutonic)', p. 753.
[4] Jón Árnason, *Þjóðsögur og Æfintýri*, Vol. iii, *Uppvakningar og
Fylgjur*, pp. 67, 68.
[5] Compare I. Reichborn-Kjennerud, *Vår Gamle Trolldomsmedisin*,
p. 53. *Standard Dictionary of the English Language*, p. 1989, Funk
and Wagnall, 1911: 'Valkyr=Norse Myth: one of the maidens that
serve in the banquets of Valhalla whence they are sent by Odin to
point out those to be slain in battle, and to bear their souls to Valhalla;
Valkyrian = martial, warlike'.
[6] With the possible exception of the *spámaðr*.

successor by the former. That the guardian spirit idea is an expression of the conception of the Norns, probably themselves originally the souls of the dead, seems clear from a glance at Snorri's Edda.[1] Like the fetch, the guardian spirit appears in dreams and visions.

The only form of guardian spirit to be found in the dreams of the Elder Edda is that of the *dísir*. In Glaumvör's dream,[2] prophetic of the slaying of Gunnarr, her husband, by King Atli, dead women, dressed in mourning, come to invite him to their benches. After telling this dream to Gunnarr she says, 'you have been bereft of your *dísir*'. He accepts this as indisputable evidence that he is to die, saying: 'It is too late to tell me—but it is very likely that we[3] shall live but a short time'.

It is interesting that, in this early example,[4] the women are specifically described as dead, whereas in the version of this dream found in *Völsunga Saga*[5] they are mentioned merely as women. In the latter Glaumvör says: 'It seemed to me that women came in; they were sorrowful, and chose you for their man.—It may be that they were your guardian spirits (*dísir*)'. That the *dísir* were originally thought of as the dead (though I have found no other instance where they are so described) is supported both by the theory of Reichborn-Kjennerud that in old folk belief the Norns were the souls of the dead,[6] and by the suggestion that *dísir* worship 'may possibly be a cult of ancestors'.[7] Later, no doubt, this

[1] *Gylfaginning*, ch. 15.
[2] *Átlamöl en grønlenzko*, *Die Lieder der Edda* (ed. B. Sijmons), p. 443, verses 25–6.
[3] Gunnarr and Högni.
[4] Finnur Jónsson places Atlamöl at about 1050. *Lit. Hist.* Vol. I, p. 313.
[5] Finnur Jónsson places Völsunga as from the last half of the thirteenth century, *ibid.* Vol. II, p. 839. Magnus Olsen, *Völsunga Saga*, p. 94: 'Enn þotti mer her inn koma konur, ok voru daprligar, ok þik kiose ser til mannz. Ma vera, at þinar disir hafe þat verit'.
[6] *Vår Gamle Trolldomsmedisin*, p. 53.
[7] B. S. Phillpotts, *Temple Administration and Chieftainship in Pre-Christian Norway and Iceland*, 1914, p. 19.

aspect of the *dísir* lost emphasis, or was more or less completely lost sight of, so that a change took place in the conception. In *Bjarnar Saga Hítdælakappa*,[1] Björn's slaying is
foretold by dreams in which 'the helmeted one, the valkyrie
of the Ruler of Heaven, invites him home'; another dream
in which the *dísir* are identified with the valkyries is found
in the *Fornaldarsögur*. Ásmundr, somewhat troubled at the
prospect of fighting eleven men single-handed on behalf of
the chiefs of Saxland, is encouraged in a dream in which
'women stood over him with weapons, and said: "How
does your looking afraid help matters? You are expected
to be the leader of others, yet you fear eleven men. We are
your spirits of prophecy, and we will grant you our protection against the men with whom you are to fight"'.[2]
This explains and presages Ásmundr's victory. Sometimes
the *dísir* have a Christian savour. Þorsteinn, in his threefold
dream,[3] prophetic of his slaying by Gilli, his thrall, sees
three women; each changes places in rotation, so that the
one who is in the middle in the first dream is before the
others in the second, and the one who is last in the first
dream is first in the third. In each case the one who comes
first says a verse, and in the second dream, it runs as follows:
'Forward to doom went the skilful judge who understood
the law. God grant the administrator of justice that he be
able to quench the ill-will (against him) before Hel, rich
in spoil, can prevail against the warrior, he who swings the
sword'.[4] Here we have what looks like a Christian senti-

---

[1] P. 77.

[2] *Ásmundar Saga Kappabana*, *Fas.* II, p. 353.

[3] *Þorsteins Saga Síðu-Hallssonar*, pp. 24–6. Although he has a
dream on each of three successive nights, they are so closely related
in content and form that they are under the heading 'Draumr Þorsteins' = Þorstein's dream, in the Saga.

[4] Translated from the Danish, Finnur Jónsson, *Skjaldedigtning*,
Vol. II, pp. 230–1: 'Frem til dommen gik den domkloge, som forstod
loven; gud unde domsfuldbyrderen det, at han kan dæmpe uviljen
(mod ham selv), för den bytterige Hel (?) faar bugt med krigeren,
ham som svinger (?) sverdet'.

ment inserted into what is intrinsically an expression of the inexorable character of the heathen idea of destiny or fate. It seems to me possible that the three women represent the three Norns, Urðr, Verðandi and Skuld (past, present and future), the difference in time being expressed by their relative positions in the successive dreams, and perhaps also by the content of the verses they say respectively. The process of Christianization is much more marked in a dream from *Heimskringla*.[1] Three maidens appear to a Danish captive, who has been freed and healed by the sainted King Oláfr Haraldsson, to reproach him for having run away from the monastery (?), thus breaking his vow to his benefactor. This is suggestive of the 'three Marys' who take the place of the Norns supposed, according to pre-Christian thought, to assist at the birth of children.[2]

The *spámaðr*[3] may be described as a masculine form of the guardian spirit. He gives information and good advice, and, by his timely warning, makes it possible for the one he serves to avoid catastrophe. In *Hrafnkels Saga Freysgoða*,[4] a man appears to Hallfreðr in a dream to warn him of danger, and to tell him to move his household. The very day he leaves a landslip comes down on the homestead. This same dream is found in *Landnámabók*,[5] but is there assigned to Hrafnkell Freysgoði,[6] the son of Hallfreðr. It is possible to argue on the basis of *Landnámabók* that the man of the dream is the god Freyr, protecting his priest, but this is unlikely, since there is evidence that, in this case, the Saga is more reliable than Landnáma.[7] Again, Sturla Sighvatsson, at a meeting of his supporters, in acquiescing in the abandonment of his plan to attack Snorri Sturluson, tells his dream

---

[1] Snorri Sturluson, *Heimskringla* (ed. Finnur Jónsson), p. 553.
[2] I. Reichborn-Kjennerud, *Vår Gamle Trolldomsmedisin*, p. 54.
[3] *Spámaðr* = prophet. The word may be applied to men who have prophetic gifts, or are wizards.
[4] Pp. 1, 2.   [5] *Hauksbók*, 1900, p. 90.
[6] Freysgoði = priest of Freyr.
[7] Wilhelm Henzen, *Über die Träume in der Altnordischen Sagalitteratur*, ch. II, p. 55; Finnur Jónsson, *Lit. Hist.* Vol. II, pp. 517–18.

of the previous night. 'A man came to him and said: "Know
that Snorri shall die (be in his coffin) before you".' He himself interprets this to mean that Snorri is to pass away before
him, thus explaining his yielding.[1] In *Þórvalds Þáttr Viðförla*
we find a *spámaðr*, here clearly worshipped as a deity, re-
treating before, and defeated by, the forces of Christianity.
When Bishop Friðrekr is engaged for three days in driving
the *spámaðr* of Koðran Eilífsson from his stronghold (a great
stone), by means of prayer, psalm-singing and the sprinkling
of holy water, Koðran has a dream on each of the three successive nights.[2] In each of these the *spámaðr* is progressively
more miserable and impotent; from exhortation and state-
ment in the first, he descends to entreaty, blame, whining
and abuse in the third. His increasing wretchedness is shown
by his equipment; his complaint that all his clothes have been
ruined is substantiated by his wearing a black and ragged
cloak. His appeal on behalf of his children, burned by the
holy water as by scalding drops, is particularly illuminating,
since it shows that an entire household is thought of as living
in the stone. When, in the second and third dreams, the
spámaðr is referred to as 'false prophet', 'fiend' and 'evil
spirit' it is plain that what is a protective and beneficent
agent in heathen philosophy is quickly degraded on coming
into contact with the new faith to the point of becoming
actively evil and even demoniacal. Its place as a good spirit, on
the other hand, seems normally to be usurped by the Christian
Saint so frequently met with in the dreams of *Biskupa
Sögur*, and possibly also by the guardian angel, as in *Eireks
Saga Viðförla*,[3] a religious tale from the fourteenth century.[4]

Now, as to the *hamingja* proper. In *Víga-Glúms Saga*,[5]
the death of his mother's father[6] is announced to Glúmr in

---

[1] *Sturlunga Saga*, Vol. I, p. 409: 'Maðr kuemi at honum ok mælti
vittu at Snori skal fyrr i kistuna enn þu'.
[2] *Þáttr af Þorvaldi Viðförla*, Bks. I, pp. 39–41.
[3] *Eireks Saga Viðförla, Fas.* III, pp. 524–6.
[4] Finnur Jónsson, *Lit. Hist.* Vol. III, pp. 87, 88.
[5] *Víga-Glúms Saga*, ch. 9, pp. 25–6.
[6] Vigfúss was a chief of Vors (Voss) in Norway.

a dream in which he sees a woman of gigantic proportions stalking along the countryside, and coming toward his homestead; he goes to meet her and invites her to his house. Glúmr himself interprets this, saying that, after his grandfather's death, his *hamingja* 'will seek to establish herself with me'[1]. That the stature of the *hamingja* may be thought of as standing in ratio to the distinction of the person to whom she is attached is clear from these words: 'the woman who was taller than the mountains as she walked must be his *hamingja*; he also was of more distinction than other men in most things'.[2] Her valkyr-aspect is shown in a verse said by Glúmr at the time when his grandfather's death is reported: 'I saw a woman wearing a helmet, come, supernatural in size, toward Eyjafjörðr..., in dreams, I thought, with dread, that the valkyrie filled the land between the mountains of the valley'.[3] (This idea of supporting battle-maiden is consistent with the fact that the dream occurs almost immediately after the dreamer's killing of Sigmundr Þorkelsson for his injustice in pasturing his livestock and harvesting grain on land belonging to Glúmr, and just before Glúmr's successful defence and counter-suit in this matter.) Another somewhat grim *hamingja*, which appears in connection with hostility and contention, is that found in the two dreams of Án the Black[4] (Hrísmagi). In the first, her action may be construed as preventing a fatal wound, and in the second, as facilitating recovery. Sometimes, like the *spámaðr*, the *hamingja* may give warning of natural calamity. In *Vatnsdæla Saga*, Þorsteinn Ingimundarson is saved from being crushed under a landslip brought down by the

---

[1] See following note.

[2] 'Mundi kona sjá hans hamingja vera, er fjöllum hærra gekk. Ok var hann um aðra menn fram um flesta hluti at virðingu, ok hans hamingja mun leita sér þangat staðfestu, sem ek em.'

[3] *Skjaldedigtning*, Vol. I, p. 112, verse 2: 'Jeg saa en kvinde med hjælm paa, komme i over-naturlig störrelse hentil Øfjorden,...jeg med frygt da syntes i drömme, at valkyrjen fyldte landet mellem dalens fjælde'.

[4] *Laxdæla Saga*, pp. 153–4, 161.

witchcraft of a sorceress through heeding the advice of 'the woman who was the guardian spirit of the family'. She appears to him in dreams on three successive nights.[1] Another dream in which the *hamingja* seems to figure is that of Þorgeirr enn Hvinverski; he is told of the identity of a man, unknown to him, whose life he is seeking on behalf of King Harald Fairhair.[2] Again, Þorgils Böðvarsson, while sleeping on a door in a refuge hut, has a dream prophetic of his slaying. He is warned by a woman who looks very sad, and says: 'There you lie, Þorgils, and you are to lie on a door once more'.[3] Here, in spite of a connection with attack, the martial quality of the valkyrie is entirely lacking. Another example of the *hamingja* is found in the good dream woman of Gísli Súrsson; the situation here is unique, since she stands in active opposition to an evil influence, the bad dream woman of Gísli. The good dream woman acquaints Gísli with the number of years he has to live; she offers him counsel as to the conduct of a good life, and she promises him her help and a joyous existence with her after death. That she exhibits a strong Christian tendency, thus showing kinship with the guardian angel, is unmistakable. Her counsels in the dream of the seven fires, while reminding us of *Hávamál*, follow the dictates of Christian creed and morality.[4] The idea that reward beyond the grave is encompassed by a comfortable and joyous counterpart to life on earth also seems to express the teaching of the new faith; however, the fact that Gísli's good dream woman takes him to her house on her grey horse, and that he is supposed to be destined to live there after death, supports the view held by Henzen[5] that she embodies one side of the valkyr-conception.[6]

[1] *Vatnsdæla Saga*, p. 90.
[2] *Landnámabók*, 1900, *Hauksbók*, p. 78.
[3] *Sturlunga Saga*, Vol. II, p. 293.
[4] *Gísla Saga Súrssonar*, pp. 50, 51.
[5] Wilhelm Henzen, *Über die Träume in der Altnordischen Saga-litteratur*, p. 78.
[6] See footnote 5, p. 30, above.

Gísli's evil genius, the bad dream woman, seems to have a more striking relationship with the martial side of the valkyr-idea; her activities are largely concerned with blood, here a symbol of violence and strife at arms. She rubs him with gore, washes him with sacrificial blood, ties a bloody bonnet on his head, and threatens to put to naught the fair promises of the good dream woman.[1] That the 'black and hideous' man who appears in the two dreams of Karkr,[2] prophetic of the slaying of Earl Hákon and his son Erlendr, is the earl's evil genius seems possible; this in spite of the temptation to the modern mind, since Karkr is himself the earl's slayer, to interpret the dream man as a personification of the dreamer's own evil intentions. That Earl Hákon does not himself have these dreams of warning may perhaps be owing to an inability to dream on his part, a condition sometimes met with, and regarded as an abnormality.

In the dreams of folklore the guardian spirit appears in two of the three forms to which we are accustomed from Old Norse. The *spámaðr* and the *hamingja*, though often displaced by the Christian angel,[3] still survive in heathen guise in a few instances, while of the *dísir*, as such, I have come upon no trace. The evil genius also seems to have vanished.

A reminiscence of the *spámaðr* in *Hrafnkels Saga Freysgoða* is found in Icelandic folklore.[4] Jón has lived and prospered at Vogar for nearly twenty years. One night he is warned by his dream man (*spámaðr*) that his good fortune will diminish if he stays in Vogar for more than the full score of years. He tells him to move to Hvalrjörður, where he will

[1] *Gísla Saga Súrssonar*, pp. 55–6, 80.
[2] Karkr is the thrall of Earl Hákon. *Heimskringla*, 1911, *Saga Óláfs Konungs Tryggvasonar*, ch. 48, p. 140.
[3] An angel appears to take the dreamer to see heaven and hell in order that he may be induced to change his way of life. See Sigfús Sigfússon, *Íslenzkar þjóðsögur og Sagnir*, Vol. I, pp. 59, 60. Also Vol. II, pp. 16–17, 19. Also E. T. Kristensen, *Danske Sagn, som de har lydt i folkemunde*, Vols. I–III, p. 301.
[4] Jón Árnason, *Þjóðsögur og Æfintýri*, Vol. III, *Galdrasögur*, p. 37.

be as successful for the next twenty years as he has been at Vogar for the last. He pays no heed to this, however, and, true to the *spámaðr's* prediction, his good fortune begins to decline at the specified time. In another story,[1] a boatman dreams that a man warns him that he is to be put to the test out beyond Holtsós. Some time later his boat is wrecked in a storm while laid up. This allays the dreamer's fear that he is to drown. He accordingly goes out in his brother's boat, and loses his life when it capsizes at the very point mentioned in the dream. A dream man of *spámaðr* type is also found in a Danish tale. A young man, just married, dreams three nights in succession that a man comes to him and tells him that he must leave home and stay away for twenty years, or else 'it will go badly with him'. He becomes so restless that he has to set out. He takes service with a farmer. After twenty years, having saved all his money meanwhile, he leaves and starts for home. When he gets there he finds that a son had been born shortly after he had left; the son has been preparing for the ministry and just at this time he is trying to replenish exhausted resources by borrowing from his father's sister. The boy is now able to finish his training with money the father has saved while away.[2]

Jón of Vogar (in addition to his dream man) also has a dream woman.[3] One day, toward the end of his life, Jón loses a silver spoon, and, though he hunts high and low, it is nowhere to be found. His *hamingja* comes to him in his sleep, and it seems to him that he asks her about the spoon. She tells him to look through his clothes. In the morning his clothes are searched, but to no avail. The next time he sees the dream woman he complains that the spoon was not where she had said, but she replies that the search was not thorough. This time he takes part in the search

[1] Jón Árnason, *Þjóðsögur og Æfintýri*, Vol. III, *Galdrasögur*, p. 21.
[2] Jens Kamp, *Danske Folkeminder*, Odense, 1877, p. 277.
[3] Jón Árnason, *Þjóðsögur og Æfintýri*, Vol. III, *Galdrasögur*, pp. 35, 36.

himself, but it is still not found. The third time she appears, he accuses her of lying and tells her never to come before his eyes again. She appears no more. The spoon is found the following winter in a pocket of Jón's fishing trousers. In another story, a wizard is said to have a dream woman.[1] One night she comes to him and asks if he would like her to tell him which woman is destined to be his wife. He accepts, and she directs him to go to a certain homestead and choose that one of the three daughters who has a birth-mark on her forehead. The marriage is happy.

It is clear from the foregoing that the matters with which the guardian spirits of folklore are concerned differ, to an appreciable extent, from those which engage the attention of their prototypes in the Sagas, and also that the attitude of the dreamers has changed. The emphasis is laid rather on danger of loss of position and prosperity than on peril of life and death. In the wizard's dream leading to his successful marriage the *hamingja* has entered even the purely domestic sphere. There is eloquent proof, too, that the guardian spirit has suffered a marked loss of prestige and has, perhaps on this account, become somewhat less effective than before. Jón of Vogar flatly ignores the advice of his *spámaðr*, to his detriment to be sure, but still with a mastery and self-sufficiency only paralleled in the Sagas by a voluntary submission to the inevitable decrees of fate, a factor surely wholly foreign to the present instance. Without the dignity of faith, and the sublimity lent by supreme sacrifice, the disregard of the guardian spirit's warning amounts to an assertion of superiority. A further step in the development of this attitude is revealed in Jón's treatment of his dream woman in connection with the lost spoon. So far from standing above him to be revered, she is subservient to his authority to the extent of being held responsible to him for her behaviour. In the case of the boatman, who shows no disposition to doubt the validity of his *spámaðr's* caution,

[1] Jón Árnason, *Þjóðsögur og Æfintýri*, Vol. III, *Galdrasögur*, pp. 245–6.

the guardian spirit fails to save the dreamer's life owing to the intervention of a minor catastrophe which is confused with the main issue. It is interesting, however, that (as we can see from Jón's dream in which his *spámaðr* shows him souls in purgatory,[1] and as is suggested by the Danish dreams of direction and warning) the old heathen conception here sometimes has sufficient vitality to keep from being itself absorbed, even when brought into close contact with Christianity, by either the guardian angel or the demon.[2] I have found no evidence that the guardian spirit of folklore is thought of as belonging to families or as passing on from generation to generation.

More sharply divergent from the guardian spirits of Old Norse are the elves which, not figuring at all in the dreams of Edda and Saga, are often of service to human beings in the dreams of folklore. Thus, an elf woman appears to a wretched little shepherd boy to help him out of his misery by telling him how to find and keep the wishing stone.[3] In the same way, a child who has been lost is found under a cliff through following the directions of a woman (elf?) who comes to one of the searchers in a dream.[4] In the luck dreams, so numerous in Danish folklore,[5] on the other hand, we have what must be one of the most conventionalized and impersonal manifestations of the guardian-spirit idea, completing an evolution from divinity to what is apparently disembodied fortune.

TROLLS

The term 'troll', though sometimes used to designate evil beings in general, or even to describe a sorcerer or sorceress, is, strictly speaking, approximately synonymous with *jötunn* (giant). Trolls may be considered, together with other

[1] Jón Árnason, *Þjóðsögur og Æfintýri*, Vol. III, *Galdrasögur*, p. 36.
[2] See p. 34 above.
[3] Oddur Björnsson and Jónas Rafnar, *Grima*, No. II, pp. 43, 45–6.
[4] Jón Þorkelsson, *Þjóðsögur og Munnmæli*, Vol. I, pp. 26–7.
[5] E. T. Kristensen, *Danske Sagn, som de har lydt i folkemunde*, Vol. III, contains many examples.

members of the lower hierarchy of the North, to have been originally the souls of the dead, in this case usually those of evil people. In later times, however, they seem to have become nature spirits.[1]

The trolls in the dreams of Old Norse literature stand in various relationships to men. They frequently seem to take the part of purposeful agents in fomenting strife or to represent a sort of incarnation of the violence of encounter at arms between opposing forces. Before the fight between Þórarinn Þórisson and Glúmr Eyjólfsson over the lawsuit in connection with the slaying of Arngrímr Þorgrímsson, Glúmr himself has a dream.[2] He sees two women, carrying a trough and sprinkling blood over all the district. This foretells the bloodshed incident to the clash between the two hostile bands. The ill-starred conflict of King Haraldr Harðráði at Stamford Bridge is predicted in the dreams of two of his followers, as they are sleeping on the ships just before sailing for England. Gyrðr dreams that he is looking toward the island (Sólundir Isles) and that a great troll woman stands there, with a short sword in one hand and a trough in the other.[3] Þórðr, in the same way, dreams that King Haraldr's fleet is approaching the coast of England, and that a great host is on the shore led by a troll woman, riding on a wolf.[4] The woman feeds the wolf a succession of corpses, throwing them into its mouth; its jaws drip with blood. Another troll woman is found in a dream of Hafliði Höskuldsson, prophetic of the fight between Þorleifr and Sturla at Kálfanes.[5] He sees a company of men led by a tall, grim-looking woman. She carries a tattered cloth from which blood drips. Then another company comes against them, and, as they fight, the troll woman brandishes the cloth over

[1] I. Reichborn-Kjennerud, *Vår Gamle Trolldomsmedisin*, pp. 57–8.
[2] *Víga-Glúms Saga*, pp. 59–60.
[3] *Heimskringla, Saga Haralds Konungs Harðráða*, pp. 500–1.
[4] *Ibid.* p. 501. Compare the troll woman, Hyrrokkin, who comes, riding a wolf, to launch the funeral ship of Baldr. *Gylfaginning*, ch. 49.
[5] *Sturlunga Saga*, Vol. I, p. 494.

their heads, decapitating each man as the tatters touch his neck. Again, two bloodstained women, sitting in a great house while blood rains in through the windows, appear to a man of Skagafjörðr in his dream prophetic of the attack on Bishop Guðmundr Arason.[1]

It is obvious that trolls in this warlike capacity have, like the *dísir* and the *hamingja*, a connection with the valkyries. But it seems to me possible that they also show a relation with an older and more primitive belief concerning the realm of the dead. If *jötunheim*, the world of giants, was originally a realm of the dead,[2] it follows that the dead must have been thought of as corpses devoured by ogres, since the word *jötunn* means 'devourer'.[3] This is precisely the idea expressed in some of the dreams. The troll woman in Þórðr's dream throws corpses into the mouth of her steed, the wolf, and says, in the verse with which she accompanies her action: '...the woman (I) slashes the men's flesh with her jaws...'.[4] In Gyrðr's dream the troll woman declares regarding carnage: '...it is profitable for me...I always support this'.[5] Profitable, I suspect, because dead bodies constitute food for giants. If the trolls were themselves originally the souls of the dead it must be that they were thought of as subsisting on the corpses of the newly dead, in the manner of cannibals, an expression of the idea that the dead, as the agents of death, swallow up the newly dead into oblivion.

That trolls might be conceived as seeking purely personal revenge is shown by Ólafr Pái's dream in *Laxdæla Saga*.[6] He has had a remarkable four-horned, ice-breaking ox slaughtered, since it had lost its natural ice-pick through old age. Its mother, a troll woman, looking very angry, appears to Ólafr and says that, since he has let her son be killed: 'You shall see your son all covered with blood by my

---

[1] *Sturlunga Saga*, Vol. I, p. 285.   [2] See pp. 40–1 above.
[3] Hastings' *Encyclopædia of Religion and Ethics*, Vol. XI, B. S. Phillpotts, 'Soul (Teutonic)', p. 754.
[4] Finnur Jónsson, *Skjaldedigtning*, Vol. I, p. 400, verse 10.
[5] *Ibid.* verse 8.   [6] *Laxdæla Saga*, p. 85.

agency; and I shall pick out the one whom I know it is hardest for you to lose'. This foretells the slaying of Kjartan by Bolli, his foster-brother, many years later.

On occasion, too, a giant may be actively friendly with a human being. When the Icelander, Molda-Gnúpr, is forced by volcanic eruptions to move to Grindavík with his family, they suffer at first from a shortage of livestock. Then Björn, one of his sons, has a dream in which a giant (bergbúi) comes to him and offers to go into partnership with him. He accepts, and shortly afterward his livestock is replenished.[1] After this Björn is called Hafr-Björn; those gifted with second sight maintain that he is accompanied wherever he goes by the land spirits (land-vættir). This may indicate that the giant, in this case, has been transformed into a full-fledged nature spirit. Another friendly troll is found in the woman who comes to Ormr Stórólfsson in his sleep to tell him the circumstances of the slaying of his foster-brother, Ásbjörn, by the giant, Brúsi, her half-brother, and to give him help in carrying out his revenge.[2] It has been suggested that daughters of giants, in contrast to mothers, show themselves friendly to people;[3] in this instance, however, it seems to me that the fact that the daughter is half human ought not to be discounted.

Only in a few instances do the trolls in the dreams of folklore show clearly their relation with those of Old Norse literature; changed conditions seem to have conspired to banish the troll as an embodiment or agent of human conflict. Of the troll as an independent being seeking personal revenge, I have but one example. In an Icelandic tale a boy of sixteen, while hunting sheep in the mountains with some others, comes upon a track of tremendous footprints stained with blood. He makes sport of them, trying to fit his gait to their size, in spite of the objections of his companions.

[1] *Landnámabók*, 1900, *Hauksbók*, p. 101.
[2] *þáttr Orms Stórolfssonar*, *Fms.* 3, pp. 222–3.
[3] Wilhelm Henzen, *Über die Träume in der Altnordischen Saga-litteratur*, p. 62.

As soon as he falls asleep in the evening he dreams that a very large woman comes to him and says that he did ill to amuse himself at the expense of a suffering giantess (*skessa*), and that before the evening of the next day there will be as much amiss with him as there was with her footprints. The next morning he is in great pain, and later one of his legs becomes contracted and stays so until the day of his death.[1] The troll as friendly to a human being is found in two Icelandic variants. In one a troll woman (*flagðkona*), whose custom it has been to steal the shepherd of a certain farmer for her Christmas dinner every year, is, nevertheless, satisfied with a gift of sheep for two years running. The third year she accepts the sheep again but carries off the shepherd as well. Apparently because of his bravery she spares his life, and after this becomes actively friendly. She gives him good advice, and magic gifts, and before he leaves she says: 'As soon as you dream of me, you must come back; by that time I shall be dead; then you shall build a howe according to the ancient custom, and take (for yourself) the treasure in the cave'. Some time later he dreams of the woman and goes back to carry out her wishes. The treasure makes him a wealthy man.[2] In the other, the tale is substantially the same, except that, in this case, the dreamer wins the affection of the giantess (*skessa*) through a gift of fish to her children when he is marooned under the mouth of her cave by a storm while on a fishing expedition.[3] In spite of the fact that both these women are specifically described as trolls (*flagðkona, skessa*), in spite of even the man-eating propensity which relates the first to the corpse-devouring trolls of the Sagas,[4] it seems to me that, as supporting and advising beings, they have affinities with the *hamingja*, except in so far as their mortality represents an approach to humanity.

For the rest, the trolls of folklore are characterized by a

[1] Jón Þorkelsson, *Þjóðsögur og Munnmæli*, Vol. I, p. 184.
[2] Jón Árnason, Vol. II, *Tröllasögur*, pp. 88–94.
[3] *Ibid.* pp. 94–103.   [4] See p. 42 above.

certain vagueness of outline and a tendency to be confused with other beings of a supernatural kind. Sometimes they are conceived as carrying out activities while they are themselves unseen by human beings, thus taking on an attribute most often associated with the elves and *huldufólk* who live in a world invisible to men not gifted with second sight.[1] Again, the troll man who appears to Bishop Guðmundr to demand that he shall not bless the mountain peak in which he lives[2] irresistibly suggests the *spámaðr* of Koðran and his reaction to the rites employed by the bishop.[3] In Danish folklore we find a troll who plays the part of a wise man in answering questions which purport to come out of dreams.[4] Sometimes, too, it is plain that the troll is drawing close to the domain of the sorcerer and the wizard; in a dream from an Icelandic story[5] a giantess sings and rocks back and forth to produce a favourable wind, and there is a dream in a Danish tale in which a bewitched princess dances with a troll man.[6] Thus, the trolls of folklore dreams, while preserving continuity with those of Old Norse literature, by reason of their greater elasticity, reach beyond them through their affinities with other more or less allied beings.

GODS

Of the heathen gods, only a few appear in connection with the dreams of Old Norse literature. The earliest reference is found in *Vegtamskviða (Baldrs draumar)*, a poem from the Elder Edda.[7] Here the gods and goddesses are assembled to discuss the dreams of ill-omen which are troubling Baldr. Then Óðinn, father of Baldr, rides away on Sleipnir, his eight-legged steed, to the gateway of Hel, where, by his spells, he raises a sibyl from her grave. In answer to his

---

[1] Jón Árnason, Vol. II, *Tröllasögur*, p. 23.
[2] *Ibid.* p. 83.   [3] See p. 34 above.
[4] Svend Grundtvig, *Danske Folkeæventyr*, Vol. I, p. 136.
[5] Sigfús Sigfússon, *Dulsýnir*, 1915, pp. 52–3.
[6] Svend Grundtvig, *Gamle Danske Minder*, No. 3, pp. 13 ff.
[7] *Vegtamskviða, Die Lieder der Edda* (ed. B. Sijmons), pp. 160–3.

question, she tells him that Baldr will be slain. The poem, at least in its present state, provides no record of the dreams themselves, so that any suggestion as to their nature must rest on free conjecture on the basis of probability; thus, Henzen supposes that they are likely to have been fetch dreams.[1] In *Gylfaginning*, too, there is mention only of 'great and perilous dreams touching his life', but the end of the story is given in the slaying of Baldr by the blind god Höðr at the mischievous instigation of Loki, and the vengeance taken upon Loki by all the Æsir.[2] This story differs from that contained and implied in *Vegtamskviða*, both as regards the measures adopted by the gods to safeguard Baldr, and the revenge exacted for his death, which, according to the prophecy of the poem, is to be accomplished by Vali, a son of Óðinn, yet unborn. On the other hand, according to Saxo, Baldr's dream, occurring three nights before his death as the result of wounds inflicted by a human rival,[3] is as follows: 'Proserpine (Hel) was seen to stand by him..., and to promise that on the morrow he should have her embrace'.[4] While it here occupies a position in the story after, instead of before, the fatal event, and while there is no evidence to show that it is not Saxo's own invention, I see no reason why this dream may not be one traditionally ascribed to Baldr, and culled by Saxo from a source now lost to us.

Just as a god is conceived as disturbed by ill-boding dreams, so also gods appear in the dreams of men.

Þórr, as the spokesman and symbol of heathendom in its losing and hopeless conflict with Christ militant, visits the newly converted Þorgils Ørrabeinsstjúpr in no less than five dreams.[5] In these he expresses a last, desperate defiance of

[1] Wilhelm Henzen, *Über die Träume in der Altnordischen Sagalitteratur*, p. 79.
[2] *Gylfaginning*, ch. 49.
[3] King Hother; he is undoubtedly Höðr in human guise.
[4] Saxo Grammaticus, Book III, p. 93.
[5] *Flóamanna Saga*, pp. 36–40.

the forces of Christianity, and his threats and their substantiation present him clearly in two distinct aspects. As a deity of the land and of husbandry, he requites Þorgils for his faithlessness to him by killing his livestock; as the god of storm (thunder god) he causes him to toss about in an extremity of privation and peril on his voyage from Iceland to Greenland. Furthermore, his activities in support of his menaces are worthy of note from another point of view. In conformity, perhaps, with the normal expectation when a declining religion first comes into contact with a new and vital faith, there is no suggestion that Þórr is not a real entity, a power to be reckoned with. He fails to be ultimately and irrevocably effective only because he is less potent than the opposing Christian Godhead. Thus, though he does not kill Þorgils, as he threatens in the second dream, it is plain that he has contented himself with bringing about the death of an old ox instead; though he does not compass the drowning of his erstwhile worshipper, he consigns him to the buffeting of the waves for many days. The idea that the holding of his property, however innocently, by the dreamer constitutes a link by virtue of which the god may continue to harass him, in spite of his disaffection, is very striking; it is only after throwing overboard a forgotten gift to Þórr, that is, surrendering a sacrifice appointed long before, that Þorgils manages to put an end to Þórr's haunting of his dreams. As we have seen occur before in the case of a beneficent spirit of heathendom brought into contact with Christianity, Þórr is degraded in the third dream to the status of 'foul fiend', and it is significant that here his proper name is not initially used; he is introduced merely as a 'large man with a red beard'. But Þórr is by no means always either so persistently belligerent or so effective. In Sveinn's dream,[1] the night before the homecoming of his brother Finnr, an ardent exponent of the new faith, Þórr has no more power, and is characterized by no more independence, majesty, or self-sufficiency than is the

[1] *Saga Ólafs Konúngs Tryggvasonar, Fms.* 2, p. 162.

spámaðr of Koðran in the face of the ministrations of Bishop Friðrekr.[1]

Víga-Glúmr, before leaving home to attend the session of the Althing at which he is sentenced to district outlawry, has a dream in which Freyr figures.[2] He sees the god, sitting on a throne by the river; many men, who declare themselves the dreamer's dead relatives, are vainly petitioning Freyr that he (Glúmr) may not be forced to leave his homestead. The suppliants complain that Freyr is obdurate, that he remembers the ox presented to him years before by Þorkell enn Hávi[3] to the end that he (Glúmr) might one day become an exile. In other words, he is unmoved by all save the offering made to him in anticipation of the performance of a definite service.

Óðinn, depicted in most poetical sources as chief among the Northern gods, does not seem to appear at all in the dreams of Old Norse literature; nevertheless, he is sometimes directly connected with them. A reflection of the remark whispered by Óðinn in Baldr's ear as he was laid on the funeral pyre, mentioned in *Vafþrúþnismál*,[4] is found in several instances. Þórr, in the fourth dream of Þorgils[5] incident to his change of faith, 'said many things to him', the nature of which we do not know. Bishop Jón dreams that, as he is saying his prayers before a great crucifix, the figure on the cross leans toward him and whispers words into his ear;[6] Bishop Guðmundr, before sailing from Norway, has a dream in which the Virgin Mary appears, and tells him 'many things he did not know before'.[7] Óðinn may also play a part in dream interpretation. Thus, he

[1] See p. 34 above.
[2] *Víga-Glúms Saga*, p. 75.
[3] At the time when he gives up his homestead under pressure from Glúmr. *Víga-Glúms Saga*, p. 28.
[4] *Vafþrúþnismál, Die Lieder der Edda* (ed. B. Sijmons), p. 68, verse 54.
[5] *Flóamanna Saga*, p. 39.
[6] *Jóns Saga hins Helga eptir Gunnlaug Múnk, Bks.* I, ch. 36, p. 246.
[7] *Guðmundar Saga, Viðbætir, Bks.* I, No. I, p. 590.

extracts from the seeress (Völva) the prophecy which elucidates Baldr's dreams,[1] and, in the shape of Hörðr, foster-father of King Ívarr, he interprets the dream prophetic of the king's death, and himself brings about its fulfilment.[2]

What factors may be supposed to govern the appearance of these particular gods in dreams, and what conception is responsible for allowing Baldr to be so far anthropo-morphized as to have dreams prophetic of his death by violence in no wise different from those which might be expected to presage the fall of a human being at the hand of a foe?

It is important to note, in the first place, that both Þórr and Freyr are closely identified with the lives of men. Þórr, as a god wielding power over land and sea alike, is intimately associated with the chief occupations and main sources of livelihood of the community at large. He is the friend of the people, as he is also the enemy of giants (*jötnar*). As the god probably most humanized, and closest to earth,[3] it is easy, in spite of poetical testimony, to credit the evidence of the Sagas that he, and not Óðinn, stands highest in the popular estimation.[4] Freyr, while sharply differentiated from Þórr in that he was originally a hostage from the Vanir,[5] shares with him a certain intimacy with the affairs of men. He is a god of fertility whose cult is centralized at Upsala, and the fact that he is said by Adam of Bremen to grant men peace and pleasure suggests that he is thought of as having the security of individuals in his gift. This, and the fact that he seems to have been taken on peregrinations (in a triumphal car) in the interest of plenty, is reflected, to my mind, in Freyr's refusal, 'as he is sitting on a throne by the river', of the petition on Víga-Glúmr's behalf.

---

[1] *Vegtamskviða, Die Lieder der Edda* (ed. B. Sijmons), p. 161, verse 7.
[2] *Sögubrot af Fornkonungum, Fas.* I, pp. 291–2.
[3] Jörð (Earth) is often regarded as the mother of Þórr.
[4] See *The Cambridge Medieval History*, Vol. II, pp. 480–95.
[5] A rival race to the Æsir.

Óðinn, by contrast, is not as widely worshipped, since, as god of the dead and later of war, he is identified with the aspirations and purposes of kings, and with the bravery and hardihood of warriors, rather than with the daily round of common life. His aspect as arch-wizard and prophet, however, constitutes perfect equipment for the rôle, on occasion, of interpreter. But if we seek to account for the appearance of gods in dreams on the basis of the extent to which they are held in popular reverence, we are also constrained to agree with Henzen when he says that the gods never figure in the dreams of persons whose faith in them is unshaken, and that it is doubt and disbelief which allows them to descend from their sublimity to the point of entering into the human land of dreams.[1] It is obvious that the five dreams in which Þórr appears to Þorgils are the expression of the succeeding stages of conflict in the dreamer's mind between the rival claims of the old and the new religions. Víga-Glúmr, too, after his dream of Freyr, 'paid less homage to him ever afterwards'.[2]

As for the dreams of Baldr foretelling his own death, it is noteworthy that there is disagreement among scholars as to the date of this poem,[3] some casting doubt on its genuine antiquity, others placing it early. If it is old, it argues for an anthropomorphic conception of the god at a very early period; if it is late, which seems to me more likely, it may be explained as an exaggeration of a tendency found in earlier models. In any case, the fall of Baldr before a foe, personal and individual tragedy though it be, only anticipates that of the majority of his fellow gods at Ragnarök, when they, with the heroes of Valhöll, make a last valiant stand against the victorious forces of destruction. But, lest

[1] Wilhelm Henzen, *Über die Träume in der Altnordischen Saga-litteratur*, p. 55.

[2] *Víga-Glúms Saga*, p. 75: '...Lézt Glúmr verr vera við Frey alla tíma síðan'.

[3] H. M. and N. K. Chadwick, *The Growth of Literature*, Vol. I, p. 248.

we misunderstand the significance of this mortality of the gods, let us quote a passage from *Wyrd and Providence in Anglo-Saxon Thought*:[1] 'The gods are mortal and subject to defeat not, surely, because the Northerners could not imagine immortality or permanent success, but because disaster is the final acid test of character. The valour of Óðinn and his peers, like the valour of human heroes, can only be proved by their fighting a losing battle, with defeat foreordained and foreknown'.

The old gods appear but rarely in the dreams of folklore; such as are found are distinguished by a very considerable retreat from their original character, though the development involved is only a further step in the evolution which is already apparent in the dreams of the Sagas themselves. If we have seen a god degraded to the rank of fiend in Old Norse literature, in folklore we find a soul-stealing devil or fiend possessing external attributes and characteristics reminiscent of Þórr or Óðinn. Thus, there is an Icelandic story of a priest's foster-son who is in the habit of calling on the devil. On one occasion he is tired of looking after the sheep at the summer pasture, and the devil comes to him in a dream to offer his services as shepherd in exchange for the surrender of his soul at the end of three years. He appears as a crafty-looking man with a red beard.[2] The dreamer is saved from having to keep his bargain only through the power invested in the Church and its clergy.

An indication that Þórr is definitely established as an evil being is inherent in the folk belief that names compounded with Þórr are 'bad omens in dreams';[3] this is so much the more striking since at least one out of every five immigrants to Iceland in heathen times had a name of which Þórr

[1] Essays and Studies, Vol. XIII, *Wyrd and Providence*, by B. S. Phillpotts, p. 13.
[2] Sigfús Sigfússon, *Íslenzkar þjóðsögur og Sagnir*, Vol. I, p. 39.
[3] 'Hörð i draumi.' Jón Árnason, *þjóðsögur og Æfintýri*, Vol. III, *Galdrasögur*, p. 20.

formed a part (Þorgils, Þorsteinn), since this was esteemed a safeguard to the bearer.[1]

As for Óðinn, I have found two versions of an Icelandic tale in which a condemned man calls on the devil to save his life, in the one instance (and this the later) because God and his angels would not hear his plea. In each case, the devil appears in a dream in answer to the man's call and bargains for his soul as the price of deliverance. He is to belong to Satan if he can catch him before the next Althing.[2] The promise given by the fiend in the dream is fulfilled at the execution through the activities of a man who bursts suddenly upon the scene. He is one-eyed, dressed in a long tunic, and carries a wand[3] (staff). Furthermore, he provides for the escape of the prisoner on a grey horse (*gandreið*).[4] Here, too, the dreamer succeeds, by placing himself under the protection of a friend, in outwitting the demon, who is thus made to serve him without compensation. In Danish folklore, one of the several variants of the theme of the set question answered by the interpretation of the fictitious dream describes the interpreter as 'den kloge mand', that is 'the wise man'.[5] This probably is a reflection of Óðinn in his capacity as a god of wisdom.[6]

In spite, however, of the fact that we are able definitely to recognize the characteristics of Þórr and Óðinn, we can also detect a certain mingling of their qualities and functions. Þórr, when he appears to offer his services as shepherd, has 'a crafty look' (*beggja blands at sjá*), a description which, while appropriate to Óðinn as god of wizardry and spells, could scarcely be applied to the honest and straightforward

[1] *The Cambridge Medieval History*, Vol. ii, p. 481.
[2] Jón Þórkelsson, *Þjóðsögur og Munnmæli*, Vol. i, pp. 105–6; and Sigfús Sigfússon, *Íslenzkar Þjóðsögur og Sagnir*, Vol. i, pp. 46–7.
[3] *Gambanteinn, reyrsprota* = wand.
[4] Witch or Wizard-ride; this is significant in view of the connection of the horse with the Æsir.
[5] Svend Grundtvig, *Gamle Danske Minder*, No. i, p. 171.
[6] *Gylfaginning*, ch. 15.

Þórr of Old Norse literature. The function of soul stealing again, whereas it seems distinctly alien to the character of Þórr, stands in direct relation with the original conception of Óðinn as a god of the dead. If, in the dreams of Old Norse literature, the heathen gods bow only before the power and majesty of 'White Christ', in folklore they are put to rout even when pitted against human wit alone.

Chapter V

SYMBOLIC IMAGES IN DREAMS (*continued*)

OBJECT SYMBOLISM

CONCRETE objects also have a wide range of significance when used in a symbolic capacity. They may stand for persons (the inanimate thus representing the animate), or provide indication of the ultimate destiny of individuals; they may offer a graphic picture of the ramifications and power of great kindreds, or embody in their finite form the glories and perils involved in success or failure.

The objects which denote persons may be described as things either prized by the dreamer on subjective grounds, or intrinsically valuable, or both. King Atli dreams of his two ill-fated sons as reeds which, in spite of his concern that nothing shall damage them, are torn up by the roots, and set before him as food.[1] Before King Sverrir's birth his mother dreams that she brings forth a glittering, snow-white stone; it throws out sparks in all directions, even after being completely covered with a cloth.[2] This foretells the greatness which is inherent in the yet unborn child, and which is to preclude the hiding of his royal parentage. In *Laxdæla Saga*,[3] the future husbands of Guðrún are represented in her four marriage dreams as a crooked hood (*krókfaldr*), a silver arm-ring, a gold arm-ring, and a gold helmet set with precious stones, respectively. It is to be noted that the nature and quality of these articles, and their fate in the

---

[1] *Guþrúnarkviþa*, II (en forma), *Die Lieder der Edda* (ed. B. Sijmons), pp. 405–6, verse 41.
[2] *Sverris Saga*, Fms. 8, pp. 7, 8. This dream may be an interpolation by Styrmer Kárason. F. Jónsson, *Lit. Hist.* Vol. II, p. 382.
[3] *Laxdæla Saga*, pp. 88–90.

dreams, express both the personal characteristics of the men involved, and their individual relations with Guðrún. The first, who is 'a rich man, and no hero', and for whom she is to care not at all, is represented as wearing apparel of a more or less usual kind. The second, whom she is to love most, is symbolized by a silver arm-ring which suits her admirably, and which is lost by a pure accident. The third, whose trickery in marrying her she is to resent, and whose death she is to compass indirectly, is depicted as a gold arm-ring, the flaws in which are clearly apparent when, 'somewhat by her negligence', it is broken; that the ring is of gold seems to be only a concession to the superiority of the Christian faith, which he is to profess.[1] The fourth, who is to be the most distinguished, and of whom Guðrún is, apparently, to stand somewhat in awe, is symbolized by a jewelled helmet of gold, so heavy that she cannot hold her head erect while wearing it.

Equally, objects may serve to indicate the fulfilment, or measure the approach, of the ultimate destiny of individuals. Thus, in Glaumvör's dream, a river whose current breaks the legs of Gunnarr and Högni foretells their slaying at the hands of King Atli.[2] The dream in which Þórhaddr stumbles over a hummock and falls is interpreted as prophetic of his death, the obstacle being described as his hummock of death (banaþúfa).[3] In the same way, the agency of a man's fate may take on a form suggestive of its relation to himself. Páll Þórðarson, in the dream which foretells his drowning, is dressed in a shining linen kirtle; the kirtle stands for the waves of the Ísafjörðr which are to envelop and engulf him.[4] The significance of a dream may also be centred in a par-

---

[1] Konrad Maurer, *Die Bekehrung des Norwegischen Stammes zum Christenthume*, Vol. I, p. 227.
[2] *Atlamöl en grønlenzko, Die Lieder der Edda* (ed. B. Sijmons), p. 443, verse 24.
[3] *Þorsteins Saga Síðu-Hallssonar*, p. 16.
[4] *Sturlunga Saga*, Vol. I, p. 106. Henzen stresses a connection between a garment and the idea of the *hamr*. *Über die Träume in der Altnordischen Sagalitteratur*, p. 43.

ticular physical characteristic or condition. Þorkell Eyjólfsson's death in the waters of Breiðarjörðr is foretold in his
dream in which his beard is so large that it reaches over all
the firth.[1] Somewhat different is the case of one of Gísli
Súrsson's dreams,[2] embracing, as it does, a considerable
future period. In this he is apprised of his death seven years
hence, through the symbolism of seven fires, one for every
year he has yet to live.

The *motif* of the family tree appears in several variants.
In a fragment of the original version of *Harðar Saga ok
Hólmverja* we find two of the simplest dreams of this kind.[3]
Signý, before the birth of her son, Hörðr, sees grow up in
her bed a beautiful, though blossomless, tree, whose branches
stretch over the homestead; again, before the birth of her
daughter, she sees another tree, large at the roots, but
withered from there up, and in very profuse bloom. Though
neither of these dreams seems to show Christian influence,
the interpretation of the second as given in the complete
Saga (later by about one hundred years) suggests that the
blossom stands for the new faith which the daughter's
descendants are to profess.[4] A tree which springs from a
thorn found in her smock figures in Queen Ragnhildr's
dream,[5] prophetic of the birth, life and future lineage of her
son, King Harald Fairhair. A black cloud, driven from the
sea toward the land, and resolving itself into a tree whose
shattered fragments drift into all the creeks and bays of the
coast, presages, in King Sigurðr's dream, the coming of
Haraldr Gilli to Norway, and the diverse fortunes of the
dynasty he is to establish there.[6] But the tree itself is not
the only symbol of descent, though the most usual. King
Hálfdan the Black has a dream in which his descendants

[1] *Laxdæla Saga*, p. 226.
[2] *Gísla Saga Súrssonar*, pp. 50, 51.
[3] *Harðar Saga ok Hólmverja*, Appendix, pp. 90, 91.
[4] *Ibid.* pp. 9–11.
[5] *Heimskringla*, ch. 6, p. 39, ch. 43, p. 69. See *Bárðar Saga
Snæfellsáss*, p. 3, for a probable reflection of this dream.
[6] *Heimskringla*, p. 547.

appear as locks of hair growing on his head in great beauty and profusion, and of many different lengths and colours; one of the locks excels all the rest and this is interpreted as representing Saint Óláfr.[1] Again, Þorgils Ørrabeinsstjúpr dreams of his future children and their kindred as five leeks sprung from one stalk, and dividing into many branches. One leek towers over his head, and is by far the finest; this stands for the sainted Bishop Þorlákr, who is to be the most distinguished of the dreamer's descendants.[2] Bishop Jón Arason's dream of laying his glove on the altar in the church at Skálholt constitutes a prophecy of the five bishops of that see descended from him.[3]

Objects are also used to give tangible or material expression to the wider considerations of victory and defeat, success or failure. A sword which breaks in battle foretells, in Þorbjörn Brúnason's dream,[4] the disaster and defeat which is to overtake the company to which he belongs in the conflict with Barði Guðmundarson and his band. A piece of sausage which he shares with his followers figures in a dream of Sturla Sighvatsson prophetic of his good fortune on an expedition against the sons of Þorvaldr.[5] King Sverrir, in encouraging his men after the farmers have made a successful sally against them, tells his dream of the night before;[6] he had an unbound book of such great size that it covered much of the country, but one section had been stolen from it. He explains the missing section as the only success which the farmers are destined to enjoy (þar hafa bændr tekit menn vára), and the rest of the book, by implication, as the measure of the ultimate victory of his forces over them. With this dream of distinctly clerical stamp we may compare that of Sturla Þórðarson in which a heavy boulder, crushing the men in its path, represents the defeat of his

[1] *Heimskringla*, pp. 39, 40.   [2] *Flóamanna Saga*, p. 46.
[3] *Sögubrot um Jón Árason, Bks.* II, p. 452.
[4] *Víga-Styrs Saga ok Heiðarvíga*, p. 70.
[5] *Sturlunga Saga*, Vol. I, p. 432.
[6] *Sverris Saga, Fms.* 8, p. 402.

side in the battle of Ørlygsstaðir, and in which a tall cross emphasizes the atmosphere of inevitable doom.[1]

In the dreams of folklore we find the same symbolic use of objects as in the dreams of Old Norse literature, though that relating to success or failure seems to disappear.

Persons portrayed as objects occur in several instances. In an Icelandic story a woman dreams that a man gives her nine fine buttons, of which, in spite of her great care, she loses all but one. The buttons are rightly interpreted as the nine children she is to have, of whom only one is to survive.[2] That the buttons are regarded as valuable in themselves, and as objects of beauty, is expressed by the attitude of the dreamer, and by their description in the dream as *mjög fagra* (very beautiful). Another woman has a dream in which her husband has lost all but three of his toes. This is prophetic of the death of seven out of their ten children.[3] Strongly reminiscent of Guðrún's third dream in *Laxdæla Saga*[4] is one found in another Icelandic tale.[5] A woman dreams that she is wearing a much treasured arm-ring, and that it breaks in two. This foretells the death of two of her daughters. A dream from the same source which, to my mind, bears an interesting, if somewhat less conspicuous, relation to the first and fourth dreams of Guðrún,[6] is ascribed to a woman of Mýrar before the birth of her daughter. She dreams that she asks a friend of hers to help her to make a cap for the child.[7] Not long afterward the friend of the dream has a son who later marries the daughter of the dreamer. The cap is thus identified with the future husband, and this explanation is explicitly supported in the interpretation by the citing of the proverb 'the man is the woman's head' (*Var*

---

[1] *Sturlunga Saga*, Vol. I, p. 515.
[2] Sigfús Sigfússon, *Íslenzkar þjóðsögur og Sagnir*, Vol. II, p. 23.
[3] *Ibid.* p. 31.
[4] *Laxdæla Saga*, p. 89.
[5] Sigfús Sigfússon, *Íslenzkar þjóðsögur og Sagnir*, Vol. II, pp. 31-2.
[6] *Laxdæla Saga*, pp. 88-90.
[7] Sigfús Sigfússon, *Íslenzkar þjóðsögur og Sagnir*, Vol. II, p. 27.

það 'kappinn', því maðurinn er kvinnunnar höfuð).[1] Though
the symbolism of the Saga dreams, which equates head-gear
with husband, thus reappears here, the interpretation constitutes a further step in its evolution, crystallized in the
popular saying 'the man is the woman's head'.

Dreams in which objects are indicative of the ultimate
destiny of individuals figure in two tales from Iceland.
A woman dreams that her dead mother comes and gives
(puts on) her a pair of glasses. One of the lenses is marked
with the numbers 1 and 7. This is understood to show the
age to which she is to live, an interpretation which is fulfilled by her death in her sixty-ninth year.[2] Another instance
concerns a man who dreams that the second hand of his
watch is lost, and that a poorer one, which moves very fast,
has taken its place. This is prophetic of the dreamer's death
within the year.[3] Though the type of object used here is
admittedly very different from that found in corresponding
dreams of Old Norse literature, the contrast veils an interesting parallel. Thus, Gísli Súrsson's dream[4] foretelling
his span of life has elements in harmony with both. The
seven fires, like the numerals on the lens, stand for a definite
number of years, and each fire, like the watch, is a concrete
symbol of division of time.

As for trees of descent in the dreams of folklore, I have
come upon them only in Irish and Scottish sources. Achta,
before the birth of Cormac, dreams that a tree whose
branches spread over all Ireland grows out of her neck,
to flourish until laid low by a huge wave of the sea; then a
second great, though somewhat less magnificent, tree springs
from the roots of the first, to be overwhelmed, in its turn,
by a blast of wind. This foretells the births, personal achieve-

---

[1] Sigfús Sigfússon, *Íslenzkar þjóðsögur og Sagnir*, Vol. ii, p. 27.
'That (the man) was the cap, because "the man is the woman's
head".' The same proverb is dramatized in a dream from an Irish
source. T. W. Rolleston, *The High Deeds of Finn*, p. 173.
[2] Sigfús Sigfússon, *Íslenzkar þjóðsögur og Sagnir*, Vol. ii, p. 32.
[3] *Ibid.* p. 34. [4] *Gísla Saga Súrssonar*, pp. 50–1.

ments, and fortunes of both Cormac and his son Cairbrie, kings of Erin.[1] In what seems to be a West Highland variant of the same tale, the mother of Conall dreams before his birth that a shoot of fir grows from the heart of the Irish king, and one from her own heart, and that they twine about each other.[2] It is noteworthy that the symbol of the tree is not, in these instances, put to quite the same use as in Old Norse literature, since it stands for an individual descendant without reference to the family he is to establish. Nevertheless, the continuity of lines of descent is clearly expressed, in the first dream, through the growth of one tree from the roots of another.

The object symbols appearing in these dreams are also of interest when considered from a more general aspect.

The genealogical tree, in the first place, seems to present a problem in respect of its origin. If we take note of its distribution within the limits set by our material, a contrast comes to light between the not inconspicuous part played by this symbol in the dreams of Old Norse literature, and its apparent absence, in any form, from those of Scandinavian folklore. While this, in itself, might not, in view of the fundamentally popular nature of folklore, be enough to place the family tree under suspicion as a native product of the North, another argument for its non-indigenous character is supplied by the use, in Skaldic poetry (sometimes as a kenning for warrior or for the martial qualities of kings and heroes),[3] of a tree quite distinct from that relating to descent. These considerations, coupled with the appearance of the genealogical tree in the dreams of Irish and Scottish sources, suggest, to my mind, that this symbol is drawn from general European, rather than specifically Norse, tradition.

[1] T. W. Rolleston, *The High Deeds of Finn*, pp. 173 ff.
[2] J. F. Campbell, *Popular Tales of the West Highlands*, Vol. II, p. 142.
[3] Finnur Jónsson, *Skjaldedigtning*, Vol. I, p. 212, verse 11, p. 235, verse 2.

Again, if it seems strange that persons and their destinies should be portrayed in terms of what we regard as the purely material, it is, perhaps, possible to explain this as a survival of a phase of primitive philosophy. Thus, it has been suggested that evidence of the persistence among the Northerners of traces of animistic belief is provided in that objects occurring in dreams are capable of interpretation.[1] This theory of the survival of animism is further supported by such a dream as that of Laxdale Guðrún in which blood comes out of the fragments of her gold arm-ring.[2] But even if this be so, it by no means follows that animism was a vital force during the period dealt with in the Sagas. It is more likely, especially in view of the intricate and highly developed character of most of the dreams concerned, that they represent a literary adaptation of a system of belief which flourished before the dawn of the Viking Age, with its emphasis on life and activity, its reluctance to recognize the dualism of body and spirit.[3]

[1] Wilhelm Henzen, *Über die Träume in der Altnordischen Saga-litteratur*, p. 42.

[2] *Laxdæla Saga*, p. 89.

[3] Compare Hastings' *Encyclopædia of Religion and Ethics*, Vol. XI, B. S. Phillpotts, 'Soul (Teutonic)', p. 755.

Chapter VI

DIRECT REPRESENTATION IN DREAMS
LIVING PERSONS, DEAD PERSONS

SYMBOLIC images, despite their great flexibility and wide range of application, do not stand alone in the dreams of Old Norse literature. There are others which, not partaking of the nature of disguise, require no interpretation.

LIVING PERSONS

It is somewhat surprising, in view of the frequency with which living persons are introduced in the guise of fetches, that they figure at all in their own shapes in the dreams of Old Norse literature; and indeed, aside from the numerous indeterminate references to dreams concerning the living,[1] we have specific record of but three of this type. Thus, Auðunn appears to his friend, Þorgils, in two dreams, once to give advice on how to conduct a duel,[2] and again to claim back his sword, and to give a gold finger-ring in part exchange.[3] Þorbjörg visits her wrath upon her faithless lover in a dream to some purpose, since he wakes with severe pain in his eyes which does not abate until he has atoned for his fickleness.[4] It is interesting to note, in connection with these dreams, how sharp is the contrast between their objective reality and the pure symbolism of the fetch image. As surely as Þormóðr wakes with a disease of the eyes, Þorgils comes out of his sleep to find the sword gone. That is, instead of giving true indication of occurrences outside it, the dream is itself the event, and the appropriate physical

---

[1] See Wilhelm Henzen, *Über die Träume in der Altnordischen Saga-litteratur*, pp. 53–4.
[2] *Flóamanna Saga*, p. 26.   [3] *Ibid.* p. 27.
[4] *Fóstbrœðra Saga*, pp. 50–1.

consequences of activities taking place within the dream frame are carried over into the waking state. The figure of the dream is no mere representation of the individual, but the person himself, who has, as it were, invaded the consciousness of the sleeper in the entirety of a corporeal presence, without losing effective contact with reality.

It has been suggested that the emphasis on the objective reality of the dream image in general, and the introduction of living persons in their own shapes in particular, are comparatively late developments,[1] and the two dreams of Þorgils, at least, offer no obstacle to this argument. The Saga in which they are found is distinctly post-classical, and probably no earlier than 1300. The case of Þormóðr's dream, however, is somewhat different. Since it is found in the Hauksbók text of the Saga, the best and most authentic version extant, it is possible that it may also have been contained in the lost original, undoubtedly classical, and from about 1200. The dream is given in much its best form in Hauksbók,[2] and there is nothing to suggest that it is not an integral part of the Saga. But if we assume it to be of such age, we are faced with the vexed question of how to account for the inclusion, in a classical Saga, of a single dream so foreign in character to the fetch type which might normally have been expected to serve a corresponding purpose. While, in the nature of things, it would seem to be

[1] Wilhelm Henzen, *Über die Träume in der Altnordischen Sagalitteratur*, pp. 54, 63.

[2] Björn K. Þorolfsson, *Fóstbræðra Saga*, pp. 73–5: '. . . þa dreymði Þormoð eina nott, er hann var a Lavgaboli, at Þorbiorg kom at hanvm, ok spvrði, hvart hann vekti eða svæfi. Hann sagþiz vaka. Hon svarar: "Þv sefr, en þat er fyri þig berr, man sva eftir ganga, sem þv vakir; eða hefir þv gefit lofkvæði þat, er þv ortir vm mik, annarri konv?" Þormoðr segir: "Eigi er þat satt", Þorbiorg mællti: "Satt er þat vist, þv hefir mitt lofkvæði gefit Þordisi Grimv dottvr, ok snvið til hennar ollvm þeim visvm, er merst heyrðu mer til. Nv mvn ek lavna þer lavsyrði þina ok lygi, sva, at þv mvndt taka avgna verk þan er bœði þin avgv skvlv vt springa, nema þv lysir þvi fyri alþyðv, at þat er mitt kvæði, ok kallir þat sva iamnan siþan". Hanvm syndiz hon miok reiðvleg, ok þickir hann sia svip hennar, er hon geck brott'.

almost impossible to substantiate any solution of the problem, there are two explanations which occur to me as possible. Such dreams may have had a place in Old Norse tradition, in spite of exclusion from the literature in obedience to a convention of Saga building, or, on the other hand, this particular example may represent a heathen and secular modification of the Christian idea that Saints, living[1] and dead,[2] manifest themselves in dreams as messengers of God.

In folklore, dreams in which living persons appear are, as might be expected, more numerous. While the wider range of experience to which they relate attests their approach to the more elastic and less conventionalized modern dream, they bear witness to affinity, both particular and general, with the dreams of Old Norse literature.

Traces of the objective reality which characterizes the dreams of the living in the Sagas, though considerably limited by rationalization, are discernible, in my opinion, in two instances. The first of these, from an Icelandic source, may well owe something to the *Fóstbrœðra Saga* dream. Thus, just as a man has fallen asleep in an upper room, it seems to him that a man with whom he has quarrelled rushes in from the stair-well, and up to the bed; he is furiously angry and attacks the dreamer, who is compelled to defend himself.[3] Here, as in the Saga, the dream is the event, but we are given no intimation of a definite and tangible physical consequence reaching beyond the boundaries of the dream. The second instance, found in a Danish story, concerns a man who has lost his glasses in the snow. He dreams that the rural postman comes into the room, lays the glasses on the table, and asks that they be handed to the dreamer when he wakes.[4] In the morning he finds that everything has taken place exactly as in his dream. This may be regarded as the converse of the dream which plays the part of, and

[1] *Hallfreðar Saga*, p. 31.   [2] See p. 68 below.
[3] Sigfús Sigfússon, *Dulsýnir*, 1915, p. 28.
[4] E. T. Kristensen, *Danske Sagn, som de har lydt i folkemunde*, Vols. I–II, pp. 566 ff., No. 345.

passes into, actuality; it amounts to the transference of a portion of reality, complete and unchanged, into the realm of the dream.

Most folklore dreams of the living, however, through performing identical functions, show a more general relation with the bulk of the dreams in Old Norse literature. That is, they are usually examples of prophecy or second sight. In an Icelandic poem, Alexander has harried the land of King Ring, and carried off his daughter. The king appears, in the aggressor's dream prophetic of the revenge to come upon him, clad in armour and carrying a sword.[1] Another dream from an Icelandic source constitutes a faithful and detailed representation of outlaws in the act of stealing sheep; this dream occurs, apparently, at the very time the theft is committed.[2] From Denmark comes the story of a man who has lost a treasured keepsake. He dreams that a friend of his comes into the room and hands him the lost gift, with the words: *Vær nu glad, her er gavtyven* ('Be of good cheer, here is the rogue'). In the morning the dreamer is wakened by the man of the dream, who turns the treasure over to him with the same exclamation.[3] Another Danish tale concerns a boy, the son of a captain. He dreams one night that he sees his father fall overboard. It is proved later that the father really fell from the boat and was drowned at the moment of the dream.[4] In the same way, a woman whose husband has suffered a scalp wound in the Schleswig war of 1848 dreams of him as coming toward her without his helmet, and with blood running down his face.[5] Again, from a Swedish source, we have the story of a young wife who has, by her marriage, incurred the enmity of her three brothers. A year after the wedding the brothers invite their

[1] Svend Grundtvig and Jón Sigurðsson, *Íslenzk Fornkvæði*, Vol. II, No. 36.
[2] Oddur Björnsson and Jónas Rafnar, *Grima*, No. IV, p. 29.
[3] E. T. Kristensen, *Danske Sagn, som de har lydt i folkemunde*, Vols. I–II, No. 344.
[4] *Ibid.* No. 339.   [5] *Ibid.* No. 347.

sister and brother-in-law to a feast. During the night she dreams that she is dancing with her younger brother, and suddenly falls dead. The next morning after breakfast the dream is fulfilled; the sister dies as the result of poison which the brothers had mixed in her drink.[1] Further, dreams of the person one is to marry, usually induced by some form of ritual, are common over a large part of northern Europe.[2]

How is the affinity of dreams directly representing the living in folklore, on the one hand with their actual prototypes in the Sagas, on the other with the principal functions of the Old Norse dream at large, to be explained? Whether or not dreams introducing the living in their own shapes constitute a departure from genuine tradition, the answer seems likely to be the same. The fact that Saga dreams of this kind are on record may be regarded as having established a precedent which facilitated their preservation in folklore in more or less the original form; it also made possible their substitution for types of dream with which the increasingly inappropriate heathen symbolism had been associated.

DEAD PERSONS

The dead in the dreams of Old Norse literature fall properly into two distinct categories, that of the heathen *draugr* and the Christian Saint. The conceptions attaching to these are fundamentally different.

The *draugr* is, apparently, thought of as having a continued existence as a unity of body and spirit. Primarily an inhabitant of his grave mound, he is also able to leave it, and thus preserve an effective relation with the living. Though most often represented as intruding upon the waking consciousness, he also appears in dreams, exerting through this medium a decisive influence on such human affairs as, for various reasons, engage his interests. The motive which

[1] August Bondeson, *Historie-gubbar fra Dal*, p. 17.
[2] Oddur Björnsson and Jónas Rafnar, *Gríma*, No. 1, pp. 37–8; Glükstad, *Hiterdals-beskrivelse*, p. 67; F. H. Feilberg, *Jul*, Vol. 11, pp. 128 ff.

governs his appearance is personal; it is calculated either to
further a project, to apprise survivors of his fate, to protect
himself and his property, to safeguard his honour or that
of his descendants, to reward kindness or wreak vengeance
for injury. Thus, the dead mother of Þorsteinn appears to
him in a dream to confirm him in his purpose of revenge
upon an enemy, and to advise him how best it may be accomplished.[1] The fatal outcome of the duel between Gunnlaugr and Hrafn is announced to their fathers through
dreams in which each contestant is seen covered with blood.[2]
In the same way, after the slaying of Þórir by the treacherous
King Ingjaldr, Án, the victim's brother, has a dream in
which he sees him (Þórir) looking very sad, and thrust
through with a sword.[3] Again, when Snorri Sturluson con-
templates moving from his homestead, Egill Skallagrímsson,
an ancestor, jealous for the family prestige and for the
integrity of his possessions, appears to a member of Snorri's
household. He declares that Snorri need not look down on
his ancestral lands, and makes disparaging comments upon
the shortcomings of the modern generation.[4] That the
draugr, like the living person, is conceived as an objective
reality, whose dream activities have consequences in the
waking state, is shown in a dream of Þorkell Geirason. Here,
a howe-dweller (*draugr*) gives him a sword which is found
by his side when he wakes.[5] Also, in *Bárðar Saga Snæfellsáss*
(admittedly very late), Bárðr, angry that his son has em-
braced the Christian faith, visits him in his sleep; he touches
his eyes with the result that his sight is lost.[6] Further, the
anxiety attributed to the *draugr* lest his howe be disturbed,
or its treasure rifled, is indicated by the lengths to which
Agnarr goes, both in bestowing fine gifts and in giving
directions for finding richer booty, in the dream in which

[1] *Þorsteins Saga Síðu-Hallssonar*, p. 20.
[2] *Gunnlaugs Saga Ormstungu*, pp. 45, 46.
[3] *Áns Saga Bogsveigis*, *Fas.* II, p. 314.
[4] *Sturlunga Saga*, Vol. I, pp. 273-4.
[5] *Reykdæla Saga*, p. 67.   [6] *Bárðar Saga Snæfellsáss*, p. 57.

he persuades his nephew to abandon the plan of looting his (Agnarr's) own grave mound.[1] On the other hand, the dead person may complain of something which interferes with his comfort. Þóra, whose husband has been buried (laid in howe) with a thrall (who killed himself rather than live after his master), has a dream in which her husband says that the presence of the thrall troubles him.[2] The dead sibyl who, in the dream of Herdís, laments the agony inflicted upon her by Christian prayer over her grave,[3] reminds us of Koðran's *spámaðr*, and his plight when brought into direct conflict with the forces of Christianity.[4]

In contrast to the *draugr* the Christian Saint, as an effluence of divine mercy, manifests himself only to chosen people. He is thus no voluntary agent entering the realm of the dream in pursuance of his own private concerns, but an instrument of God charged with His work and dependent upon His grace. Under the designation of 'Saints' dream' belong those, in particular, in which dead Bishops of Iceland and other Saints perform miracles of healing and deliverance on behalf of such persons as call upon the powers of Heaven for help. The numerous dreams of this type, products of the teaching of the mediæval church, are so foreign to the old philosophy of the North that it seems needless to examine them in any detail.[5]

But, in spite of the sharp differentiation between the *draugr* and the Saint, we have some dreams in which the boundaries of the two seem to overlap. The sainted Knut Lavard appears to his son to assure him of victory, and to give him directions as to how to draw up his line of battle.[6] Though he expresses the idea that victory rests with God, the Saint is primarily the father who has come to give advice in the same manner as the *draugr* in *Þorsteins Saga Síðu-*

[1] *Þorskfirðinga Saga*, pp. 8–9.
[2] *Landnámabók*, 1900, *Hauksbók*, p. 24.
[3] *Laxdæla Saga*, p. 236.   [4] See p. 34 above.
[5] Compare W. Henzen, *Über die Träume in der Altnordischen Saga-litteratur*, p. 32.   [6] *Knytlínga Saga*, *Fms.* 11, p. 371.

Hallssonar.[1] Before King Óláfr Haraldsson definitely re-
solves to return to Norway to regain his throne from the
usurper, he has a dream in which King Óláfr Tryggvason
discourages him from accepting dominion in a foreign land,
and incites him to go back and fight for his ancestral kingdom.[2] Though he supports his exhortation with references
to King Óláfr's divine right to sovereignty over Norway,
he is, at the same time, expressing his own patriotism for
the country he has himself formerly ruled, and his interest
in the fortunes of a kinsman. In the same way, a personal
motive seems to be responsible for the dream in which the
Christian, Sigmundr Brestisson, appears to his widow to
allay her unjust suspicion of a son-in-law. The idea that the
dream figure represents an emanation of God's mercy is
here, perhaps, somewhat modified by the older conception
of independence. Sigmundr reveals himself, apparently, like
a *draugr*, of his own volition, but only 'by the permission
of God Himself'.[3]

The number of dead persons who appear in the dreams
of folklore is much greater than in Old Norse literature,[4]
and the boundaries between the heathen and Christian categories are less sharply defined. The Saint, as such, is almost
entirely displaced by what we may term 'the lay Christian',
while the *draugr*, perhaps because of freedom from the
restraint imposed by ecclesiastical influence, tends to become
proportionally more prominent.

The *draugr* dreams of folklore are closely linked with
those of Old Norse literature. Thus, a young man, prostrated
with grief at the death of his mother, dreams, while sleeping
on her grave, that she comes and takes him to task for his
weakness in allowing himself to be incapacitated by his
sorrow; she declares that he shall have no rest until he has
shaken off his lethargy and freed a princess from the bounds

[1] See p. 67 above.
[2] *Heimskringla, Saga ins Helga Óláfs Konungs*, p. 377.
[3] *Færeyinga Saga*, p. 75.
[4] If the Saints' dreams of *Biskupa Sögur* be disregarded.

of sorcery.[1] This may be compared with the dream in *þorsteins Saga Síðu-Hallssonar* in which the mother gives advice, and suggests a course of action, for the benefit of her son. Instances in which the *draugr* announces his own fate are also met with. When Sigfús Eiríksson has been murdered, through the treachery of a jealous rival, he appears, covered with blood, to a relative, and says: 'See, kinsman, how my friend Jón has dealt with me now'.[2] In the same way, a man who has been slain by his guide is seen in a dream with blood dripping from his forehead.[3] Nor has the conception of the *draugr* as an agent producing physical effects reaching beyond the limits of the dream died out. A woman dreams that her brother appears to tell her that he is dead; since she will not believe him, he grows angry and pinches her arm so that the bruise is seen in the morning.[4] Again, a man who has been so ill-advised as to use a gravestone for his forge, is visited in his sleep by the dead man; he inflicts an incurable injury on the offender's leg.[5] The *draugr* as the protector of his howe, and of the treasure it contains, figures in several dreams. Thus, a man engaged in breaking into a howe is, in consequence, molested by the *draugr*. After each day's work, the dead man appears, twice threatening him with destruction if he does not stop digging, and, a third time, almost bringing about his death.[6] We also have ample evidence that the comfort of the dead man in his grave is of paramount importance. A man newly buried appears to his daughter to complain that his feet are cold. It is found that his toes have been left uncovered.[7] Another man appears to a friend on his wedding night to

[1] Sigurður Nordal and Þórbergur Þórðarson, *Gráskinna*, 1928, pp. 30–1.
[2] Sigfús Sigfússon, *Íslenzkar þjóð-Sögur og Sagnir*, Vol. I, p. 83: 'Sjáðu frændi, hvernig hann Jón vinur minn fór nú með mig'.
[3] *Ibid.* Vol. III, p. 42.
[4] Jón Árnason, *þjóðsögur og Æfintýri*, Vol. III, *Galdrasögur*, p. 22.
[5] *Ibid.* Vol. II, *Draugasögur*, p. 15.
[6] *Ibid.* pp. 85–6.
[7] Sigurður Nordal and Þórbergur Þórðarson, *Gráskinna*, 1931, p. 20.

beg that his bones may be assuaged of their thirst for brandy. He is satisfied when a keg is poured over his grave.[1] In all these cases the *draugr*, the dead man who lives in his grave, is substantially the same as in Old Norse literature.

As for the 'lay Christian', he is often hard to distinguish clearly from the *draugr*; the two tend to merge into each other. Thus, if one dead man attempts to assure the prosperity of his daughter by telling her, in a dream, where his treasure is buried,[2] another appears to his friend to entreat him to take his treasure from its hiding-place and keep it, in order to release him (the dead owner) from the necessity of visiting it every night.[3] This conception of the dead man forced to return to his secret hoard savours, to my mind, of the Christian doctrine of expiation. The idea of atonement is also expressed in connection with a dream in which a skeleton rewards a girl for helping it to make its peace with an enemy; it directs her to the finding of a purse as recompense for the peace which only the reconciliation could have brought.[4] Further, the dead Christian may be much concerned with the importance of being buried in consecrated earth. A girl who has committed suicide, and whose grave is, accordingly, to be outside the churchyard, appears to the priest who is to bury her to threaten that, if he does not place her body in consecrated ground in defiance of his superiors, he shall have a grave as unhallowed as her own.[5] This anxiety regarding burial is probably responsible for many of the dreams in which victims of the sea or the blizzard make known to survivors where their bodies may be found;[6] in these we have what looks like a Christian variation of the dream in which the Saga *draugr*, primarily to the end that he may be avenged, discloses his fate at the

[1] Jón Árnason, *Þjóðsögur og Æfintýri*, Vol. II, *Draugasögur*, p. 22.
[2] Jón Þorkelsson, *Þjóðsögur og Munnmæli*, Vol. I, p. 345.
[3] *Ibid.*
[4] *Ibid.* p. 417.
[5] Jón Árnason, *Þjóðsögur og Æfintýri*, Vol. II, *Draugasögur*, pp. 112–13.
[6] *Ibid.* pp. 6–7, 116; Vol. III, *Galdrasögur*, p. 149.

hands of a foe. Again, a dead person may appear in dreams to announce his own lot in the next world, or, more rarely perhaps, to induce a living relative or friend to mend his ways so that his soul may not be lost.[1] The 'lay Christian', in so far as he may be defined on the basis of these dreams, would seem to be distinguished from the *draugr* chiefly by his attitude of detachment towards the affairs of this world.

[1] Jón Þorkelsson, *Þjóðsögur og Munnmæli*, Vol. i, pp. 12, 13; Jón Árnason, *Þjóðsögur og Æfintýri*, Vol. ii, *Draugasögur*, p. 8; Hylten-Cavallius, *Wärend och Wirdarne*, Vol. i, pp. 356 ff.

Chapter VII

CONCLUSION

IT may be of value, in summing up, to emphasize certain points which have emerged in the course of this study. In the first place, we have distinct evidence of progression from the heathen to the Christian mode of thought in Old Norse literature, and of the further development of this process in folklore, while, at the same time, we also find a reflection in folklore of the heathen point of view. This interplay of factors not exclusively the product of their respective periods suggests that, although conditions of life dictate to an appreciable extent the content of the dream, they do not entirely determine its character.

The vehicle of the dream is the image, and, for this reason, the imagery employed in individual dreams may be regarded as of especial significance, that relating to the sphere of the animate or supposed animate being perhaps the most interesting.

One of the most striking developments of this dream representation is the way in which, in folklore, all the supernatural or extra-human beings of heathendom tend either to become confused with each other, and with various members of the Christian hierarchy, or to be completely ousted by the latter. The fetch disappears almost completely in folklore, and is apparently largely replaced by an independent substitute which has the Christian attribute of immortality. The guardian spirit is found in two feminine forms and one masculine. Of these, the *dísir*, possibly the oldest, go out entirely in folklore, while the *hamingja* and the *spámaðr* undergo three types of modification: they may merge with the guardian angel and the Saint, or become subservient to human beings, or, as foils to Christian forces, degenerate into demons. Trolls, like the guardian spirits, were probably originally the souls of the dead. Of the three relationships in which they stand to men in Old Norse literature, two, and these the more human and friendly, persist in folklore. Thus, while the troll as an incarnation of violence disappears altogether, as a compound of a human being actuated by motives of personal revenge or gratitude, and a nature spirit, it survives; certain of its characteristics also suggest affinity with the guardian spirit and the elf. Such gods as figure in dreams are those at once the most prominent and the most closely connected with the everyday needs and occupations of men. Even these, which we might expect to retain their individuality to the last, tend, in the degraded demon form in which they appear in folklore, to become confused with each other. Throughout the course of this evolution we may trace the progressive decay of the fabric of pre-Christian philosophy and religion.

Since we have only one trustworthy example in Old Norse literature of a living human being appearing to a dreamer in his own shape, it is hard to decide how far this mode of representation is indigenous, and how far it departs from the essential character of the Old Norse dream. Living persons figure more frequently in folklore dreams, which, by performing an identical function, attest their relationship with the bulk of the dreams of Old Norse literature; they also, in reflecting a wider range of experience, show kinship with the less conventional and more flexible modern dream.

The dead appearing in the dreams of Old Norse literature fall into two distinct categories, the heathen *draugr* (who was apparently originally thought of as inhabiting his burial mound), and the Christian Saint; sometimes, however, the latter, contrary to the Christian idea of dependence on the will and grace of God, manifests himself independently and in pursuit of his personal interest, and thus seems to encroach on the sphere of the *draugr*. The two categories (heathen and Christian) are less sharply defined in folklore, where the dead play a much more prominent part, and the balance between them, in favour of the Christian in Old Norse literature, is here much more even. At the same time, it is interesting to note that, whereas the absence of Saints, as such, testifies to the fundamentally secular character of folklore, the greater number of dead reflects the emphasis on the future life consistent with the Christian ideal.

Images falling outside the sphere of the essentially animate also play a part in dreams. Objects have a wide range of significance when employed symbolically, and their use in folklore is substantially the same as in Old Norse literature. Gifts of various kinds, both material and otherwise, may be acquired through the medium of the dream. The influence of conditions of life is plain in that such gifts in Old Norse literature are chiefly designed to facilitate combat, while in folklore they are largely concerned with proficiency in peaceful vocations or economic prosperity.

At this point we may ask how far the dream in Old Norse literature is a pure literary convention, and how far it is the expression of actual experience. In answering this question we must first take into account the fact that, in contrast to that of announcement and direction in folklore, the prophetic dream tends to predominate in Old Norse literature. This circumstance may be taken, from one point of view, as an argument against its genuineness, and, from another, as evidence in support of its authenticity. Although the prophetic dream constitutes an effective and convenient means of welding together literary material, it is, in view of its emphasis on fate and its intense interest in the things of this world, a typical expression of heathenism; in the same way, the folklore dream, with its insistence on the life beyond the grave, is, as has been mentioned before, a characteristic product of the Christian ideal. The introduction, in a few instances, of ritualistic beliefs and practices in connection with the dreams of Old Norse literature[1] is, to my mind,

[1] *Heimskringla, Hálfdanar Saga Svarta*, p. 39. Hálfdan sleeps in a pig-sty to induce his dream of the locks of hair. *Jómsvikinga Saga, Fms.* 11, p. 4. King Gormr builds a new house in which he sleeps

another factor which vouches for their basis in human experience. It is difficult to imagine that such rituals could be inserted solely in order to serve a literary end; on the other hand, it is conceivable that, as beliefs and practices current at the time, they may have slipped into a context to the development of whose central theme they are not strictly indispensable. This idea is borne out by the wide use of ritual in folklore,[1] which, as the spontaneous expression of the popular mind, is not primarily or consciously literary.

Although no attempt has been made to estimate to what extent specific dreams in Old Norse literature are employed as literary conventions, it is suggested that the simpler the dream, the more likely it is to approximate to real experience. On the other hand, there is no doubt that the later and more intricate dream becomes a recognized and highly developed device for the better unification of material. Thus tradition, whose roots are fixed in remote antiquity, is, under the influence of the demands of literature, concentrated into a strong and well-formed trunk, to be later released in spreading branches which still thrive in the light of the present day.

for three winter nights, in order to induce the dreams he has in connection with his marriage with Þyri. *Sögubrot af Fornkonungum*, *Fas.* II, p. 288. King Hrœrekr's wife, Uðr, prepares for him in the middle of the floor a new bed with new bedclothes, in order to induce his dream about King Ívarr and his doings.

[1] Jón Árnason, *Þjóðsögur og Æfintýri*, Vol. II, *Draugasögur*, p. 114. A man puts the clothes of someone about whom he is anxious to dream under his pillow. In Norwegian, Swedish, Danish and German folklore we find rituals in connection with dreams relating to marriage. Cp. *Norsk Folkeminnelag*, No. 12, p. 31; J. Wahlfisk, *Bidrag til Södermanlands äldre kulturhistorie*, Vol. VIII, p. 92; F. H. Feilberg, *Jul*, Vol. II, p. 128.

Appendix

TEXTS AND TRANSLATIONS

Áns Saga Bogsveigis. (*Fas.* II, pp. 293–321.)

Fas. II, p. 314. The night before King Ingjaldr's men came to land, Án had this dream:

'Mér þótti Þórir hér kominn daprlegr mjök; enn ávalt hefir hann komit er mik hefir dreymt hann; enn eigi vilda ek at þeir fœri erindislausir, er hann fœra hingat með slíku móti, (er mér) segir hugr um, því hann sýndist mér allr blóðugr, ok stóð sverð í gegn um hann.'

'I thought Þórir had come here, very sorrowful, and he has always come when I have dreamed of him. Furthermore, I do not want those who have brought him to have done so in vain, if he is in the condition I suspect, because he seemed to me to be all bloody, and a sword pierced him through.'

Ásmundar Saga Kappabana. (*Fas.* II, pp. 339–56.)

Fas. II, p. 353. On the eve of a conflict against eleven warriors, Ásmundr Kappabani had the following dream:

...konur stóðu yfir honum með hervápnum ok mæltu: 'Hvat veit óttabragð þitt? Þú ert ætlaðr at vera forgangsmaðr annarra, enn þú óttast ellifu menn; vér erum spádísir þínar ok skulum þér vörn veita móti mönnum þeim, er þú átt við at reyna'.

...women stood over him with weapons, and said: 'How does your looking afraid help matters? You are expected to be the leader of others, yet you fear eleven men. We are your spirits of prophecy, and we will grant you our protection against the men with whom you are to fight'.

Atlamöl en grønlenzko. (Ed. Sijmons, *Die Lieder der Edda,* pp. 437–64.)

Die Lieder der Edda, pp. 440–1, verses 15, 16, 18. Before Högni's death at the hands of King Atli, his wife, Kostbera, told him the following dreams:

'Blæjo hugþak þína brinna í elde, hryte hör loge hús mín í gøgnom.'

'I thought your sheet was consumed in flames, the fire leapt high through the house.'

'Björn hugþak inn komenn,
　　bryte upp stokka,
hriste svá hramma,　　at vér
　　hrædd yrþem;
munne oss mörg hefþe,　　svát
　　mættem etke:
þar vas ok þrömmon　　þeyge
　　svá lítel.'

'I dreamed a bear had come in, broke up the benches, shook his paws so we were afraid; took many of us into his mouth so that we were helpless; there was no little tumult and noise.'

'Örn hugþak inn fljúga　　at
　　endlöngo húse:
mon oss drjúgt deilask,　　dreifþe
　　oss öll blóþe;
 .　　 .　　 .　　 .
hugþak af heitom　　at være
　　hamr Atla.'

'I thought an eagle flew in along the house; he will deal hardly with us, sprinkled us all with blood
 .　　 .　　 .　　 .
from his behaviour I thought it was the shape of Atli.'

Die Lieder der Edda, pp. 442–3, verses 22, 24, 25. Before Gunnarr's death, his wife, Glaumvör, told him the following dreams:

'Blóþgan hugþak mæke　　bor-
　　enn ór serk þínom
—ilt es svefn slíkan　　at segja
　　nauþmanne—,
geir hugþak standa　　í gøg-
　　nom þik miþjan,
emjoþo ulfar　　á endom böþom.'

'I thought a bloody sword was sticking out of your tunic—it is hard to tell one's husband such a dream; I thought a spear was thrust through you; wolves howled at both ends of the spear.'

'Ó hugþak inn rinna　　at
　　endlöngo húse,
þyte af þjóste,　　þeystesk
　　of bekke,
bryte fötr ykra　　brøþra hér
　　tveggja,
gørþet vatn végja:　　vesa mon
　　þat fyr nekkve.'

'I thought a river ran the length of the house, roaring with violence, rushed toward the benches, broke the legs of both you brothers; the water was not to be stemmed; that must mean something.'

'Konor hugþak dauþar　　koma
　　í nött hingat,
vére vart búnar,　　vilde þik
　　kjósa,
byþe þér bráþlega　　til bekkja
　　sínna:
ek kveþ aflima　　orþnar þér
　　díser.'

'I thought dead women came here in the night, dressed in mourning; they wanted to choose you, asked you at once to their benches. I say your guardian spirits have forsaken you.'

Bárðar Saga Snæfellsáss.

P. 3. When Bárðr was eighteen years old he had this
dream:

…hann dreymdi at honum þótti tré eitt mikit koma upp í eldstó fóstra síns Dofra. Þat var harðla margkvíslótt upp til limanna. Þat óx svá skjótt, at þat hrökk upp í hellisbjargit, ok því næst út í gegnum hellisgluggann. Þar næst var þat svá mikit, at brum þess þótti honum taka um allan Noreg, ok þó var á einum kvistinum fegursta blóm, ok váru þó allir blómamiklir. Á einum kvistinum var gullslitr.

…he dreamed that a great tree sprang up in the hearth of Dofri, his foster-father. It was very much branched up to the twigs and grew so quickly that it reached the rock of the cave, and shot out through its opening. Next it became so large that the top seemed to him to spread over all Norway, and though one of the branches carried the most beautiful of the blooms, they were, nevertheless, all in profuse blossom. One of the boughs was the colour of gold.

P. 57. The night after Gestr had become a Christian he
dreamed as follows:

…dreymdi hann, at Bárðr faðir sinn kæmi til hans ok mælti: 'Illa hefir þú gert, er þú hefir látit trú þína, þá er langfeðgar þínir hafa haft, ok látit kúga þik til siðaskiftis sakir lítilmensku, ok fyrir þat skaltu míssa bæði auga þín'. Tók Bárðr þá at augum hans heldr ópyrmilega ok hvarf síðan.

…he dreamed that Bárðr his father came to him and said: 'You did wrong when you abandoned your faith, the one which your forefathers have held, and let yourself be cowed into a change of faith on account of paltriness; for that you shall lose both your eyes'. Then Bárðr touched his eyes rather roughly and (then) vanished.

Bjarnar Saga Hítdælakappa.

P. 59. On the eve of his encounter with Þórðr Kolbeinsson,
Björn had the following dream:

'Mér þótti, sem sex menn sætti mik, ok þótti mér nær þurfa handa við; kann vera, at þá hafir þú heyrt til mín.'

'It seemed to me that six men set upon me, and I thought I had need of hands (near); it may be that it was then you heard me.'

P. 77. Before his death at the hands of Þórðr Kolbeinsson, Björn was haunted by this dream:

'Undr's ef ekki benda
(opt vakir drengr at lengrum);
ógn hefk firða fregna—
framvísar mér dísir;
þvít armleggjar orma
Ilmr dagbœjar hilmis
heim ór hverjum draumi
hjalmfaldin byðr skaldi.'

'It would be remarkable if foresighted guardian spirits do not give me a sign—I have heard the threats of the men; often I keep awake so much the longer—because a helmeted woman from the King of Heaven invites the Skáld in each dream.'[1]

'Þetta hefir mik oft dreymt', sagði hann, 'ok nú með mestu móti í nótt.'

'I have often dreamed this', he said, 'but last night it appeared with the greatest persistence of all.'

Eireks Saga Víðförla. (*Fas.* III, pp. 517–27.)

Fas. III, pp. 524–6. When in Odáinsakr Eirekr Víðförli had this dream:

...vitraðist honum ungr drengr vænn ok bjartr. Sá mælti við hann: 'Mikil er staðfesti trúar þinnar (Eirekr); seg þú mér, hversu þér lízt land þetta'. Eirekr segir: 'Óskavel, ok hverju landi líkar mér þetta betr, enn hverr er þú, er við mik mælir ok skilr mikit okkra vizku, er þú kennir mik ok nefnir mik á nafn, enn ek veit eigi hverr þú ert'. Þá lét hinn ungi maðr við hann blíðlega ok mælti: 'Ek er engill guðs ok einn af þeim er varðveita Paradísar hlið. Ek var nær staddr, þá er þú strengdir heit at fara suðr í heim at leita Ódáinsakrs; eggjaða ek þik at sigla til Miklagarðs, ok at guðs forsjá ok mínum vilja tók þú skírn, ok firir því tel ek þik sælan at þú hlýddir þrifsam-

...a young man, handsome and bright-looking, appeared to him. He said: 'The steadfastness of your faith is very great, Eirekr; tell me how you like this land'. Eirekr said: 'Very much indeed, and it seems better to me than any other; but who are you who speak to me? there is a great disparity in our knowledge since you know me and call me by name, while I do not know who you are'. At that the young man seemed pleased and said: 'I am an angel of God, and one of those who guard the gates of Paradise. I was near when you made your vow to go South through the world in search of the field of the un-dying; it was I who influenced you to sail to Mikla-

[1] All Skaldic verse is translated from the Danish of Finnur Jónsson's *Skjaldedigtning.*

legum áminningum Grikkjako-
nungs ok ráðum ok tókt innsigli
af honum ok þótt þik í hinnihelgu
Jórdan. Enn dróttinn sendi mik
til þín; ek er varðhaldsengill
þin(n) ok ek hefi þér hlíft á sjó
ok á landi ok við allri háskasam-
legri ferð, ok varðveitt þik við
öllum illum hlutum. Enn vér
erum eigi menn, heldr andar
byggjandi á himneskri fóstrjörðu.
Enn sá staðr, er þú sér hér, er
sem eyðimörk til at jafna við
Paradisum, enn skamt heðan er
sá staðr ok fellr þaðan á sú er þú
sátt. Þangat skulu öngvir lífs
koma, ok skulu þar byggja andar
réttlátra manna. Enn sá staðr, er
þú hefir hittan, heitir jörð lifandi
manna. Enn áðr þú komt hingat,
bauð guð oss at vakta þenna stað
ok sýna þér jörð lifandi manna
með nokkurri mynd ok gera þér
veizlu ok launa þér erfiði þitt'.
Þá spurði Eirekr engilinn: 'Hvar
býr þú?' Engillinn segir: 'Vér
búum á himni þar sem vér sjám
andlegan guð, enn fyrir nauðsynja
sakir eru(m) vér sendir í heimin(n),
at veita mönnum vóra þjónustu,
sem þú skalt eigi gruna'. Eirekr
mælti: 'Hvat heldr upp þessum
stöpli, er mér sýnist hanga í
lofti?' Engillinn segir: 'Einn
saman guðs kraftr heldr honum
upp: af slíkum táknum skaltu eigi
gruna, at guð skapaði alla hluti
af öngu'. Eirekr mælti: 'Eigi
skal ek þat gruna'. Engillinn
spurði Eirek: 'Hvórt viltu hér
vera eftir, eða viltu aftr hverfa
til þinna áttjarða'. Eirekr svarar:
'Aftr vil ek hverfa'. Engillinn
mælti: 'Hví viltu þat?' Eirekr
segir: 'Því at ek vil segja kun-
ningjum mínum frá slíkum dýr-

KD

garðr, and it was by God's foresight and my will that you
accepted baptism, and I count you
blessed because you gave heed
to the wholesome warning and
advice of King Grikkja, and received his seal, and bathed in the
holy Jordan. The Lord sent me
to you; I am your guardian
angel; I have protected you on
sea and land and in all dangerous
undertakings, and defended you
against all evils. But we are not
men, rather spirits inhabiting a
heavenly country. Nevertheless,
the land you see here is as a
desert in comparison with Paradise, but that is but a short way
off, and from there flows the
river which you saw. No one
living shall come thither, and the
souls of righteous men shall
people it. The place which you
have come upon is called "the
land of living men". Before you
came God commanded us to
watch this place, and show you
the land of living men in some
way, to prepare a feast for you
and reward your labours'. Then
Eirekr asked the angel: 'Where do
you live?' The angel answered:
'We live in Heaven where we see
God in the Spirit, but for necessity's sake we are sent into the
world to serve men, as you must
not doubt'. Eirekr said: 'What
holds up this steeple which seems
to me to hang in the air?' The
angel said: 'God's power alone
holds it up; from such tokens
you shall not doubt that God
created everything out of nothing'.
Eirekr replied: 'I will not doubt
it'. The angel asked Eirekr: 'Do
you wish to stay here, or would

6

ðarverkum dróttinslegs máttar, enn ef ek kem eigi aftr, þá munu þeir því trúa, at ek hafi illum dauða dáit'. Engillinn mælti: 'Þó at nú sé goðablót á Norðrlöndum, þá mun þó koma sú tíð, at þat fólk mun leysast frá villu ok man guð kalla þat til sinnar trúar. Nú gef ek þér leyfi til aftr at fara til þinna ættjarða ok at segja þínum vinum frá guðs miskunn, þeirri sem þú sátt ok heyrðir, því skjótara munu þeir trúa guðs erindi ok öllum hans boðorðum, er þeir heyra þvílíkar sögur. Vertu oft á bænum; mun ek þá koma eftir þér nokkurum vetrum síðar ok bera önd þína í fagnað ok varðveita bein þín í þeim stað, sem þau skulu dóms bíða. Vertu hér sex daga ok hvílið ykkr ok takið síðan leiðarnest ok farið norðr aftr síðan'. Nú þótti honum engillinn hverfa sér at sýn. Eirekr gerði alla hluti, sem engillinn hafði boðit honum, um þarvist sína ok brottferð.

you rather go back to the land of your inheritance?' Eirekr answered: 'I should like to go back'. The angel said: 'Why do you want to do that?' Eirekr answered: 'Because I want to tell everyone I know of such glorious proofs of God's might as I have seen, and if I do not come back they will think that I have suffered an evil death'. The angel said: 'Though there be now sacrifice to the gods in the Northlands, yet the time will come when that people shall be freed from error; God will call them to His faith. I release you to go to your ancestral lands, and to tell your friends of God's mercy, according to what you have seen and heard, for they will have faith in His message and accept all His commandments the more quickly for hearing such tales. Be often at prayers; I shall come after you some years later and carry your spirit to a place of joy, burying your body where it is to await the day of doom. Stay here and rest for six days, and then take food and go back to the North'. Then it seemed to him that the angel disappeared from his sight. Eirekr did everything according as the angel had directed, both as to his staying and his going away.

Færeyinga Saga.

P. 75. While Þuríðr Þorkelsdóttir was harbouring reproachful thoughts about her son-in-law, Leifr, she had this dream:

...dreymði, at Sigmundr Brestisson bóndi hennar kœmi at henni, er verit hafði. Hann mælti til

...she dreamed one time that Sigmundr Brestisson, her late husband, came to her and said:

hennar: 'Þat er sem þér sýniz, at ek er hér kominn ok er mér þetta lofat af guði sjálfum, segir hann en haf eigi harðan hug né illan á Leifi mági þínum þvíat honum mun auðit verða at reka yðvarra skamma'.

'It is as you think; I have come here, and it is by the permission of God Himself. Do not harden your heart and think ill of Leifr, your son-in-law, for he is destined to take vengeance for your shame'.

Flóamanna Saga.

P. 26. Þorgils Örrabeinsstjúpr was advised in a dream by his friend Auðunn to fight a duel with a *berserkr*:

...dreymdi Þorgils, at Auðunn vinr hans kœmi at honum ok mælti: 'Þú sefr, en jafnt mun vera sem þú vakir; þú skalt á hólm ganga við berserk þenna, því at þér unnum vér sœmdar; en Svartr þessi er bróðir minn, ok er hann mér þó ekki þarfr; er hann ok et mesta illmenni. Þess spyrr hann jafnan, þá er hann háir hólmgöngur, þann, er hann skal berjask við, hvárt hann hafi sverðit Blaðni, en ek gaf þér þat, en þú skalt fela þat í sandi, ok seg honum, at þú vitir eigi hjölt sverðs þess fyrir ofan jörð'. Eftir þat hvarf Auðunn í brott.

...Þorgils dreamed that Auðunn, his friend, came to him, and said: 'You are asleep but it shall go for the same thing as if you were awake; you shall fight (the) duel with this *berserkr*, because we are jealous for your honour. Svartr is my brother, but he does me no good for all that; he is a very wicked man. When he is to fight a duel he always asks his adversary whether he has the sword (called) Blaðnir; I gave you it, but you must bury it in the sand and tell him that you do not know that the hilt of this sword is above ground'. Then Auðunn vanished.

P. 27. On another occasion Þorgils dreamed as follows:

Eina nótt kom Auðunn at Þorgilsi ok heimti at honum sverðit Blaðni—'en ek mun fá þér fyrst öxi, en innan lítils tíma gott sverð'. Þorgils kvað hann víst hafa skyldu sverðit. Auðunn bað hann hafa þökk fyrir ok gaf honum fingrgull. En er Þorgils vaknaði, var sverðit brottu ok þótti honum svipr at.

One night Auðunn came to Þorgils and claimed the sword Blaðnir—'but I will first get you an axe, and, in a little time, a good sword'. Þorgils said that he might certainly have his sword. Auðunn thanked him for that and gave him a gold finger-ring. When Þorgils awoke the sword was gone and he took the loss much to heart.

Pp. 36–40. Not long after his conversion to Christianity, Þorgils Örrabeinsstjúpr had the following five dreams:

i

Hann dreymdi eina nótt, at Þórr kœmi at honum með illu yfirbragði, ok kvað hann sér brugðizk hafa, 'hefir þú illa ór haft við mik,' segir hann, 'valit mér þat er þú áttir verst til, en kastat silfri því í fúla tjörn, er ek átta, ok skal ek þér í móti koma'. 'Guð mun mér hjálpa,' segir Þorgils, 'ok em ek þess sæll, er okkart félag sleit.'

He dreamed one night that Þórr came to him, looking very angry; he said that he had disappointed him. 'You have behaved badly as concerns me,' said he, 'you have chosen for me the worst that you have, and have thrown the silver which was my possession into a foul pool, and I will requite you.' 'God will help me,' said Þorgils, 'and I am happy that our partnership is broken.'

ii

Enn barsk Þórr í drauma Þorgilsi, ok sagði, at honum væri eigi meira fyrir at taka fyrir nasar honum en galta hans. Þorgils kvað guð mundu því ráða. Þórr heitaðisk at gera honum fjárskaða. Þorgils kvaðsk eigi hirða um þat.

Again Þórr appeared to Þorgils in his dreams and said that it would be no harder for him to strangle him than his boar. Þorgils said that was in God's hands. Þórr threatened to harm his livestock. Þorgils said he did not care about that.

iii

Þorgils bíðr nú byrjar ok dreymir, at maðr kœmi at honum, mikill ok rauðskeggjaðr ok mælti: 'Ferð hefir þú ætlat fyrir þér, ok mun hon erfið verða'. Draummaðrinn sýndisk honum heldr grepplegr. 'Illa mun yðr farask', segir hann, 'nema þú hverfir aftr til míns átrúnaðar; mun ek þá enn til sjá með þér.' Þorgils kvaðsk aldri hans umsjá hafa vilja, ok bað hann brott dragask sem skjótast frá sér; 'en mín ferð teksk sem almáttigr guð vill'. Síðan þótti honum Þórr leiða sik á hamra nökkura, þar sem

Þorgils waited for fair winds, and dreamed that a man came to him, large and with a red beard; he said: 'You intend to go on a journey and it will be a difficult one'. The dream man seemed rather frowning. 'It will go hard with you', said he, 'unless you turn back to my service; if you do that I will again take care of you.' Þorgils said he would never want his protection and bade him leave him at his swiftest, 'but my voyage will prosper as Almighty God wills'. After that he thought Þórr led him to cer-

sjóvarstraumr brast í björgum, —'í slíkum bylgjum skaltu vera ok aldri ór komask, utan þú hverfir til mín'. 'Nei,' sagði Þorgils, 'far á brott enn leiði fjandi; sá mun mér hjálpa, sem alla leysti með sínum dreyra.' Síðan vaknar hann.

tain crags where the surge of the sea broke on the rocks—'You shall be in such waves and never get out of them unless you turn to me'. 'No,' said Þorgils, 'go away, you foul fiend; He will help me who redeemed all mankind with His blood.' After that he awoke.

iv

Þorgils dreymdi, at enn sami maðr kœmi at honum ok mælti: 'Fór eigi sem ek sagða þér?' Þórr talaði þá enn margt við Þorgils, en Þorgils rak hann frá sér með hörðum orðum.

Þorgils dreamed that the same man came to him and said: 'Has it not gone as I told you?' Then Þórr talked a great deal to Þorgils, but he repelled him with hard words.

v

...dreymdi Þorgils, at sami maðr kom at honum ok mælti: 'Enn sýndisk þat hversu trúr þú vart mér er menn vildu á mik kalla, en ek hefi beint nú fyrir þínum mönnum, ok eru nú komnir at þrotum allir, ef ek dugi þeim eigi, en nú muntu taka höfn á sjau nátta fresta, ef þú hverfr til mín með nökkuri alvöru'. 'Þótt ek taka aldri höfn,' segir Þorgils, 'þá skal ek þér ekki gott gera.' Þórr svarar: 'Þótt þú gerir mér aldri gott, þá gjalt þú mér þó góz mitt'. Þorgils hugsar hvat um þetta er, ok veit nú, at þetta er einn uxi, ok var þetta þá kálfr, er hann gaf honum. Nú vaknar Þorgils.

...Þorgils dreamed that the same man came to him and said: 'It is to be seen how true you were to me when people wanted to call on me; I have just been with your men and they have come to their last resource now if I do not help them; nevertheless, you shall come to harbour in seven days time if you turn to me with any earnestness'. 'Though I never come to harbour,' said Þorgils, 'I shall do you no service.' Þórr answered: 'Though you never do me service, yet you must yield up my property'. Þorgils thought over what this might be, and he remembered that it was an old ox which he had given to him when it was a calf. Then Þorgils awoke.

P. 42. Þórey Þorvarðssdóttir once told Þorgils that she had had the following dream:

...hon kvaðsk sjá fögr heruð ok menn bjarta.

...she saw a fair country-side and people radiantly bright.

P. 45. Before his successful law-suit with Ásgrímr Elliða-Grímsson, Þorgils had this dream:

'Ek þóttumk á þingi vera á Íslandi; þótti mér sem vit Ásgrímr Elliða-Grímsson togaðim eina hönk, ok misti hann.'

'I thought I was at the Thing in Iceland and that Ásgrímr Elliða-Grímsson and I were pulling against one another on a rope, and that he lost.'

Pp. 45–6. On the night following his dream about Ásgrímr Elliða-Grímsson, Þorgils had two dreams concerning his future wife and his descendants, respectively:

i

'Ek þóttumk heima vera í Traðar-holti, ok var þar fjölment; ek sá álft eina ganga eftir gólfinu ok var blíðari við aðra en mik; þá hristi ek hana, ok var hon þaðan af miklu betr til mín.'

'I thought I was at home in Traðarholt, and that there were many people there. I saw a swan go up the floor and she was more friendly to others than to me; then I shook her and after that she was much more kind to me.'

ii

'Enn dr ymdi mik', segir Þorgils, 'at ek væra heima í Traðarholti; ek sá á kné mínu enu hœgra, þar váru vaxnir fimm hjálmlaukar saman ok kvísluðusk þar af margir laukar, ok ofarlega yfir höfuð mér bar einn laukinn; en svá var hann fagr sem hann hefði gullslit.'

'Again I dreamed', said Þorgils, 'that I was at home in Traðar-holt; I looked at my right knee and there were five leeks grown out of one stalk; many leeks branched off, and one leek towered over my head which was so beautiful as to look golden.'

P. 46. Þorleifr Þorgilsson once related this dream to his father:

'Þat dreymdi mik, faðir, at mér þótti Þórný systir mín gefa mér osthleif, ok váru af bárurnar.'

'I dreamed, father, that Þórný, my sister, gave me a cheese, and that all the crust was off.'

Fóstbræðra Saga.

Pp. 50–1. After Þormóðr Kolbrúnarskáld had changed a poem, originally com osed in honour of Þorbjörg, so that it appeared to be in praise of Þórdís, he had this dream:

...hann dreymir, at Þorbjörg Kolbrún kemr at honum, ok spurði hann, hvárt hann vekti

...he dreamed that Þorbjörg Kolbrún came to him and asked him whether he was awake or

eða svæfi. Hann kvaðst vaka.
Hon mælti: 'Þér er svefns, enn
þat eitt berr fyrir þik, at svá
mun eftir ganga, at þetta beri
fyrir þik vakanda. Eða hvat er
nú—hvárt hefir þú gefit annarri
konu kvæði þat er þú ortir um
mik?' Þormóðr svarar: 'Ekki er
þat satt'. Þorbjörg mælti: 'Satt
er þat, at þú hefir mitt lofkvæði
gefit Þórdísi Grímudóttur, ok
snúit þeim erendum, er mest
váru ákveðin orð, at þú hefðir
um mik ort kvæðit, því(at) þú
þorðir ekki, lítill karl, at segja
satt til, um hverja konu þú hefðir
ort kvæðit. Nú mun ek launa
þér því lausung þína ok lygi, at
þú skalt nú taka augnaverk mikinn
ok strangan, svá at bæði augu
skulu springa ór höfði þér, nema
þu lýsir fyrir alþýðu klækiskap
þínum þeim er þú tókt frá mér
mitt lofkvæði og gaft annarri
konu. Muntu aldrigi heill verða,
nema þú fellir niðr þær vísur,
er þú hefir snúit til lofs við
Þórdísi, enn takir þær upp, er þú
hefir um mik kveðit—ok kenna
ekki þetta kvæði öðrum enn
þeim, sem ort var í öndverðu'.
Þormóði sýndist Þorbjörg vera
reiðuleg ok mikilúðleg; þyykist
nú sjá svipinn hennar, er hon
gengr út.

asleep. He said he was awake.
She said: 'You are asleep, but
what you dream will come to pass
as if you were awake. But how
is it now—have you given what
you composed for me to another
woman?' Þormóðr answered:
'That is not true'. Þorbjörg said:
'It is true that you have given
the poem dedicated to my praise
to Þórdís Grímudóttir and have
re-adapted the lines which gave
most evidence of your having
composed it for me, because you
did not dare, paltry man, to tell
the truth as to which woman you
had made the poem to. Now, I
will reward you for your false-
ness and lying so that you shall
be seized by a very severe pain
in the eyes, so violent that both
your eyes will burst out of your
head, unless you declare before
the people your baseness in taking
from me my poem of praise and
giving it to another woman. You
shall never be cured unless you
drop the verses you have turned
to the praise of Þórdís and restore
those you composed upon me—
and do not assign this poem
otherwise than at first'. It seemed
to Þormóðr that Þorbjörg was
angry-looking and imposing; he
thought he saw a fleeting glimpse
of her as she went out.

P. 115. When Þormóðr was lying exhausted on a skerry in
the neighbourhood of Vík, a farmer living there, called Grímr,
had the following dream:

...maðr kom at honum, vænn
ok merkilegr, meðalmaðr vexti,
riðvaxinn ok herðimikill. Sá
maðr spurði Grím, hvárt hann

...a man came to him who was
handsome and distinguished, of
average height, square built and
broad-shouldered. The man asked

vekti eða svæfi. Hann svaraði: 'Ek vaki. Enn hverr ert þú?' Draummaðr segir: 'Ek em Óláfr konungr Haraldsson; ok er þat erendi mitt hingat, at ek vil, at þú farir eftir Þormóði hirðmanni mínum ok skáldi ok veitir honum björg, svá at hann megi þaðan komast, sem hann liggr, í skeri einu skamt frá landi. Nú segi ek þér þetta til merkja, at þat er satt er fyrir þik berr, at sjá maðr útlendr, er verit hefir á vist með þér í vetr ok Gestr nefndist, hann heitir Steinarr, ok er kallaðr Helgu-Steinarr; hann er íslenzkr maðr, ok fór hingat til Græn- lands, at hann ætlaði at hefna Þorgeirs Hávarssonar; enn þó at Steinarr sé garpr mikill ok harð- fengr, þá mun honum verða lítils af auðit um hefnd eftir Þorgeir, ok mun hans harðræði annarsstaðar meira fram koma'. Nú er Óláfr konungr hafði svá mælt, þá vaknar Grímr.

Grímr whether he was awake or asleep. He answered: 'I am awake; but who are you?' The dream man said: 'I am King Óláfr Haraldsson, and my errand here is that I want you to go for Þormóðr, my man and court- poet (*skáld*), and give him help so that he may get away from where he lies on a skerry not far from land. Now, as a sign that what is appearing before you is true, I will tell you that the foreign man who has been staying with you during the winter, and who has been calling himself Gestr, is (really) named Steinarr or Helgu-Steinarr. He is an Ice- lander, and came here to Green- land because he intended to avenge Þorgeirr Hávarsson; but, though Steinarr be a great and valiant hero, he is destined to do little concerning the vengeance for Þorgeirr, and his hardihood will come more into its own elsewhere'. When King Óláfr had spoken thus, Grímr awoke.

Gísla Saga Súrssonar.

P. 29. Before Vésteinn was slain, Gísli had the following dreams:

Þat dreymdi mik ena fyrri nátt, at af einum bœ hröktist höggormr ok hjoggi Véstein til bana. En ena síðarri nátt dreymdi mik, at vargr rynni af sama bœ ok biti Véstein til bana.'

'I dreamed the night before last that a viper wriggled from a certain homestead and struck Vésteinn dead. Last night I dreamed that a wolf ran from the same homestead and bit Vésteinn to death.'

P. 51. Gísli once dreamed as follows:

...'dreymdi mik nú, at ek þóttumk ganga at húsi einu, eða skála, ok inn þóttumk ek ganga húsit, ok þar kenda ek marga nni, frændr mína ok vini. Þeir

...'I dreamed that I went to a house or hall and I thought I went in and recognized within there many people, my relatives and friends. They sat by the fires

sátu við elda ok drukku, ok váru sjau eldarnir—sumir váru mjök brunnir, en sumir sem bjartastir. Þá kom inn draumkona mín en betri ok sagði, at þat merkti aldr minn, hvat ek ætta eftir ólifat; ok hon réð mér þat, meðan ek lifða, at láta leiðast (enn) forna sið ok nema enga galdra né forneskju, ok vera vel við daufan ok haltan ok fátœka ok fáráða.'

and drank, and the fires were seven. Some of them were much burned out, but some were at their brightest. Then my better dream woman came in and said that that marked the years of my life which I still had left unlived; she counselled me, while I lived, to shun the ancient faith, to take up no charms or witchcraft, and to be kind to the deaf, the halt, the poor and the helpless.'

Pp. 55–6. One winter Gísli dreamed much:

Ok kemr nú á þref um draumana, þegar er lengir nóttina; ok kemr nú en verri draumkonan at honum, ok gerast nú svefnfarar harðar, ok segir nú eitt sinn Auði, hvat hann dreymdi, er hon spurði eftir, ok kvað þá vísu:

And the dreams come again as soon as the night lengthens, and now the worser dream woman comes to him again, and he sleeps restlessly; one time he told Auðr what he dreamed when she asked, and said a verse:

'Villa os, ef elli
oddstríðir skal bíða
(mér gengr Sjöfn í svefna
sauma) mínir draumar.
(Stendr) eigi (þat þeygi),
þorn-reið, bragar greiði
öl-Nanna selr annars
efni (mér fyr svefni).'

'My dreams deceive me if the warrior (I) is to grow old; a woman appears to me in my sleep; she gives the poet no reason to assume otherwise, woman; but that does not at all prevent me from sleeping well.'

Ok nú segir Gísli, at konan sú en verri kemr oft at honum ok vill jafnan ríða hann blóði ok roðru ok þvá honum í, ok lætr sér il(li)lega. Þá kvað hann enn vísur:

And now Gísli says that his worser dream woman often comes to him and constantly wants to rub him with gore and sacrificial blood and to wash him in it, and behaves hideously. Then he recited (these two) verses:

'Eigi verðr enn (orða
oss lér um þat) borða
Gefn drepr fyr mér glaumi,
gótt ór hverjum draumi;
kemr þegars ek skal blunda
kona við mik til funda,
oss þvær unda flóði,
öll í manna blóði.'

'Yet again not all dreams stand for something good; the woman kills my joy; about this I find words; a woman, all sprinkled with blood, comes to me as soon as I want to sleep, and washes me in blood.'

'Sagt hefk enn frá órum
oddflaums viðum draumi,
Eir (varðat mér) aura
(orðfátt) es munk láta.
Verr hafa vápn snerru
vekjendr, þeirs mik sekðu,
brynju hatrs ens bitra
beiðendr, ef nú reiðumk.'

'Still I have told the warriors
of my dream, woman, about
my death. Words were not
lacking to me; the warriors,
those cravers of the sharp
sword, who made me an out-
law are in a worse position if
I should grow angry now.'

Pp. 73–4. Gísli once dreamed:

...at konan sú en betri kom at
honum; hon sýndist honum ríða
grám hesti, ok býðr honum með
sér at fara, til síns innis, ok þat
þekkist hann. Þau koma nú at
húsi einu, því er nær var sem höll
væri, ok leiðir hon hann inn í
húsit, ok þóttu honum þar vera
hœgendi í pöllum, ok vel um
búit. Hon bað þau þar vera, ok
una sér vel—'ok skaltú hingat
fara, þá er þú andast', sagði hon,
'ok njóta hér fjár ok farsælu'. Ok
nú vaknar hann.

...that his better dream woman
came to him; she seemed to ride
on a grey horse and invited him
to go with her to her house, and
that he accepted. They came to a
house which seemed as if it were
a hall, and she led him into the
house and it seemed to him that
there were cushions on the seats
and that it was comfortable. She
prayed that they should both stay
there and be well content—'and
you shall go hither when you die,
and enjoy prosperity and happiness'. Then he awoke.

He said some verses concerning his dream:

'Fleins bauð með sér sínum
saum-Hlakk gráum blakki
þá vas brúðr við, beiði,
blíð lofskreyti, ríða.
Mágrundar kvaðsk mundu,
mank orð of þat skorðu,
hyrjar Sól af heilu,
hornflœðar, mik grœða.'

'The woman invited the warrior to ride with her on her
grey horse; then she was
friendly to the *skáld*; the
woman said that she would
cure me without treachery;
I remember her words about
this.'

'Dýr lét drápu stjóra
dís til svefns of vísat
lœgis elds, þars lágu
(lítt týnik því) dýnur.
Ok með sér en svinna
saums leiddi mik Nauma,
sákat hól í hvílu,
hlaut skald sæing blauta.'

'The glorious woman gave the
skáld a seat where down-
pillows lay; I do not forget it;
and the wise woman brought
me there with her; the *skáld*
got a soft bed; I saw no rough-
ness in it.'

'Hingat skalt, kvað hringa
Hildr at Óðar gildi,
gleinþolla með fullu
fallheyjaðr of deyja;
þá munt, Ullr, ok Ilmi
ísungs féi þvísa,
þat hagar okkr til auðar,
ormláðs, fyrir ráða.'

'Here you shall surely come at
your death, warrior, said the
woman to the poet; then,
generous man, you will own
this property and the woman;
it will be for our good fortune.'

Pp. 80–1. Not long before Gísli's death:

...kom at honum draumkonan
sú en verri ok mælti svá: 'Nú
skal ek því öllu bregða, er en
betri draumkonan mælti við þik;
ok skal ek þess ráðandi, at þér
skal þess ekki at gagni verða, er
hon hefir mælt'. Þá kvað Gísli
vísu:

'Skuluða it, kvað skorða
skapkers, saman verða.
sva hefr ykkr til ekka
eitrs goð munar leitat:
allvaldr of hefr aldar
erlendis þik sendan
einn ór yðru ranni
annan heim at kanna.'

'Þat dreymdi mik enn', sagði
Gísli, 'at sjá kona kom til mín,
ok batt á höfuð mér dreyrga
húfu, ok þó áðr höfuð mitt í
blóði, ok jós á mik allan, svá at
ek varð alblóðugr.' Gísli kvað
vísu:

'Hugðak þvá mér Þrúði
þremja hlunns ór brunni
Óðins elda lauðri
auðs mína skör rauðu,
ok (hraun kveifar) hreifi
hand væri því bandi
báls í benja éli
(blóð rauð) vala slóðar.'

...his worser dream woman
came to him and spoke in this
manner: 'Now I shall change
all that which the better dream
woman told you, and I shall take
care that what she has said shall
not be to your gain'. Then Gísli
said a verse:

'You two are not to be together, said the woman; thus
God has determined your
happiness to be mixed with
grief. God has sent you away
from your home alone to visit
the other world.'

'I dreamed again', said Gísli,
'that that woman came to me and
bound a gory bonnet on my head,
and before this washed my head
in blood and bespattered me so
that I was all bloody.' Gísli recited a verse:

'I dreamed that the woman
washed my head red for me in
blood drawn from the well of
blood, and the woman's hand
was all bloody; the blood dyed
my head red.'

Ok enn kvað hann:
'Hugðak geymi-Göndul[1]
gunnaldu mér falda
of rakskorinn reikar
rúf dreyrugri húfu;
væri hendr á henni
í hjörregni þvegnar.
Svá vakði mik Sága
saums ór mínum draumi.'

And again he said:
'I dreamed that the blood-keeping woman put a bloody bonnet on my evenly cut hair, and that her hands were washed in blood; at this the woman waked me from my dream.'

P. 81. Not long before his end Gísli dreamed:

'Þat dreymdi mik, at menn kœmi at oss, ok væri Eyjólfr í för, ok margt annarra manna, ok hittumst vér, ok vissa ek, at áburðir urðu með oss. Einn þeira fór fyrstr, grenjandi mjök, ok þóttumst ek höggva hann sundr í miðju, ok þótti mér vera á honum vargs-höfuð. Þá sóttu margir at mér; ek þóttumst hafa skjöldinn í hendi mér ok verjast lengi.'

'I dreamed that enemies came upon us, and Eyjólfr was on an expedition with a great number of other men; we met, and I knew that battle-charges would come against us. One of them came first, howling furiously, and I thought I cut him asunder in the middle; he seemed to have a wolf's head. Then many attacked me; I thought I had the shield in my hand and defended myself a long time.'

Gunnlaugs Saga Ormstungu.

Pp. 3–4. Þorsteinn Egilsson once had this dream prophetic of the unhappy destiny of his daughter:

...'ek þóttumst heima vera at Borg ok úti fyri karldurum, ok sá ek upp á húsin, ok á mæninum álft eina væna ok fagra, ok þóttumst ek eiga ok þótti mér allgóð. Þá sá ek fljúga ofan frá fjöllunum örn mikinn. Hann fló hingat ok settist hjá álftinni ok klakaði við hana blíðlega, ok hon þótti mér þat vel þekkjast. Þá sá ek, at örninn var svarteygr ok járnklær váru á honum; vasklegr sýndist mér hann. Því næst sá ek fljúga annan fugl af suðrætt. Sá fló hegat til Borgar, ok settist á húsin hjá álftinni ok vildi þýðast hana. Þat var ok örn mikill.

...'I was at home in Burg, out-side the men's door, and looked up at the house, and saw on the house-ridge a swan, beautiful and fair to look at; I thought it was mine and it seemed very good to me. Then I caught sight of a great eagle flying down from the mountains. He flew hither and settled near the swan and cackled to her graciously, and she appeared to be well pleased. Then I saw that the eagle was black-eyed and that he had iron claws; I thought him valiant. Next I saw another bird fly from the south quarter, and he flew hither to Burg, and settled

---

[1] Göndul is a valkyr-name; its use here emphasizes the battle-maiden aspect of Gísli's bad dream woman.

Brátt þótti mér sá örninn, er fyri var, ýfast mjök, er hinn kom til, ok börðust þeir snarplega ok lengi, ok þat sá ek, at hvárumtveggja blæddi; ok svá lauk þeira leik, at sinn veg hné hvárr þeira af húsmæninum, ok vóru þá báðir dauðir. Enn álftin sat eftir hnipin mjök ok daprleg. Ok þá sá ek fljúga fugl ór vestri; þat var valr. Hann settist hjá álftinni ok lét blítt við hana, ok síðan flugu þau í brott bæði samt í sömu ætt, ok þá vaknaða ek.'

by the swan and wanted to court her. That was also a great eagle. Soon it seemed to me that the eagle who had first come ruffled up much at the other one's coming, and they fought sharply and long, and I saw that they both bled; their sport ended so, that they fell one on each side of the house-ridge, and were then both dead. But the swan stayed in her place, and was drooping much and sad. Then I saw a bird fly from the west; it was a hawk. He sat beside the swan and behaved lovingly to her, and afterwards they both flew away together into the same quarter, and then I awoke.'

Pp. 45–6. At the time of Gunnlaugr's fatal duel with Hrafn, Gunnlaugr's father, Illugi, had this dream:

Honum þótti Gunnlaugr at sér koma í svefninum, ok var blóðugr mjök, ok kvað vísu þessa fyri honum í svefninum. Illugi mundi vísuna, er hann vaknaði, ok kvað síðan fyri öðrum:

He thought that Gunnlaugr came to him in his sleep, and was very bloody, and said this verse before him:

.   .   .   .

'Vissak Hrafn, en Hrafni
hvöss kom egg í leggi,
hjaltugguðum höggva
hrynfiski mik brynju,
þás hræskári hlýra
hlaut fen vaða benja;
klauf gunnsproti Gunnar
Gunnlaugs höfuð runna.'

'I noticed that Hrafn cut me with the hilted sword, but the sharp edge bit Hrafn's legs, when the raven waded in blood; the warrior's sword cleft Gunnlaugr's head.'

P. 46. At the same time, Hrafn's father, Önundr, had this dream:

Önund dreymdi at Hrafn kvæmi at honum ok var allr alblóðugr. Hann kvað vísu þessa:

Önundr dreamed that Hrafn came to him and was all bloody. He said this verse:

'Roðit vas sverð, en sverða
sverð-Rögnir mik gerði,

'The sword was dyed red beyond the sea and the warrior

(vóru reynd í rondum
randgölkn) fyr ver handan;
blóðug hykk í blóði
blóðgögl of skör stóðu
sárfíkinn hlaut sára
sárgammr enn ó þramma.'

wounded me. The swords were
tried in the shields. I think the
bloody ravens stood in blood
over their heads; the wound-
lusting raven still waded in
blood.'

Guþrúnarkviþa, II (en forna). (*Die Lieder der Edda*, pp. 395–407.)
Die Lieder der Edda, pp. 405–6, verses 39–43. Before the
slaying of his two sons, King Atli told his wife, Guðrún, that he
had had the following dreams:

...'hugþak þik, Guþrún
          Gjúkadótter,
læblöndnom hjör   leggja mik
          í gøgnom.'

...'I thought, Guþrún Gjúkadóttir, that you thrust me through
with a poisoned sword.'

'Hugþak hér í túne   teina
          fallna,
þás ek vildak   vaxna láta:
rifner meþ rótom,   roþner
          í blóþe,
borner á bekke,   beþet mik
          at tyggva.'

'I thought that reeds had fallen
here in the homefield which I had
wanted to let grow; torn up by
the roots, reddened in blood,
brought to the table, offered me
to eat.'

'Hugþak mer af hende   hauka
          fljúga
bráþalausa   bölranna til;
hjörto hugþak þeira   viþ
          hunang tuggen,
sorgmóþs sefa,   sollen blóþe.'

'I thought hawks flew, hungry,
from my hand to the domain of
the dead; I seemed to eat their
hearts with honey, swollen with
blood, sorrowful of mind.'

'Hugþak mer af hende   hvelpa
          losna,
glaums andvana,   gylle báþer;
hold hugþak þeira   at hræom
          orþet,
nauþogr nae   nýta skyldak.'

'I thought moaning whelps slipped
out of my arms, both howling;
it seemed to me that their bodies
became corpses; reluctant, I was
forced to eat of it.'

Hallfreðar Saga.
P. 31. While Hallfreðr was abroad, he married a woman who
was not a Christian. Some years later he had this dream:

...honum þótti Óláfr konungr
koma til sín ok var reiðulegr ok
kvað hann mjök kasta kristni

...he thought that King Óláfr
came to him; he looked angry
and said that he had fallen off

sinni—'far á fund minn ok lið
þitt'. Hallfreðr andvarpaði mjök
er hann vaknaði.

greatly from the Faith—'come
to visit me with your following'.
Hallfreðr was panting hard when
he woke.

Harðar Saga ok Hólmverja.

P. 66. Before Hörðr and his band attempted to 'burn in'
Indriði, Þorbjörg of Indriðastaðir had the following dream:

...áttatigir varga rynni þar at
bœnum, ok brynni eldr ór munni
þeim, ok væri einn í hvítabjörn,
ok þótti hann heldr dapr, ok
dvöldust nökkura stund á bœnum,
ok runnu síðan vestr ór garði á
hól nökkurn, ok lögðust þar niðr.

...eighty wolves ran to the
homestead with fire flaming out
of their mouths; among the pack
was a white bear and he seemed
rather sad; he stayed some time
about the house, and then ran
westward out of the homefield to
a certain hillock and lay down
there.

P. 90. Before the birth of her son, Hörðr, Signý had this
dream:

...hun þottiz sia tre micít í hvilu
þeirra grimkels oc fagrt mioc oc
suo micklar limar aa at henni
þotti taka yfir husin aull en eingi
á blomin á límunum.

...she thought she saw a great
tree in the bed of Grímkell and
herself, very beautiful and with
such large limbs that they seemed
to stretch over all the house(s);
but there were no blossoms on
the branches.

P. 91. Later, before the birth of her daughter, Þórbjörg, Signý
had the following dream:

...hun sæi tre eitt mest...nidr
i rotum en uisnadi vpp þadan oc
veri a blomi (mikill).

...she saw a tree largest...
down by the roots but withered
from there up, and in very profuse bloom.

Hávarðar Saga Ísfirðings.

P. 59. Before his farm was attacked, Atli of Otradalr had the
following dream:

...'ek þóttumk ganga út ór
útibúrinu, ok sá ek, at vargar
runnu sunnan á völlinn átján
saman, en fyrir vörgunum rann

...'I thought I went out from
the out-house and I saw that
wolves ran to the field, from the
south, eighteen together, and in

refkeila ein; þat var svá slœglegt kvikindi, at slíkt hefi ek aldri sét fyrri; þat var ógurlegt mjök ok illilegt; þat skygndist víða ok á öllu vildi þat auga hafa, ok öll sýndust mér dýrin grimmleg. En er þau váru komin heim at bœnum, þá vakti Torfi mik, ok veit ek víst, at þat er manna hugir.'

front of the wolves ran a vixen. It was so sly a creature that such I have never seen before; it was very awful and ill-looking; it spied about far and . wide and wanted to have its eye on everything, and all the beasts seemed fierce to me. But when they had got to the stead Torfi woke me. I know for a certainty that these are the fetches (*hugir*) of men.'

P. 60. Before the attack on Atli's homestead, Þorgrímr Dýrason dreamed:

'Heima hefi ek verit um hríð á bœnum, ok er svá vilt fyrir mér, at ek veit ekki frá mér, en þó munum vér heim ganga at bœnum. Ætla ek, at vér skulum brenna þá inni; þykkir mér þat skjótast mega yfir taka.'

'I have been at the house awhile, but it is so bewildering to me that I do not know how it will turn out; nevertheless, let us go to the homestead. I think that we should burn them in the house; that seems to me the quickest way we may accomplish our purpose.'

Heimskringla.

Saga Hálfdanar Svarta, p. 39. Ragnhildr, wife of Hálfdan the Black, king of Norway, had this dream before the birth of her son, King Harald Fairhair:

...hon þóttisk vera stödd í grasgarði sínum ok taka þorn einn ór serk sér, ok er hon helt á, þá óx hann svá, at þat varð teinn einn mikill, svá at annarr endir tók jörð niðr ok varð brátt rótfastr, ok því næst var brátt annarr endir trésins hátt í loptit upp; því næst sýndisk henni treit svá mikit, at hon fekk varla sét yfir upp; þat var furðu digrt; inn nezti hlutr trésins var rauðr sem blóð, en þá leggrinn upp fagrgrœnn, en upp til límanna snjóhvítt; þar váru kvistir af trénu margir stórir, sumir ofarr, en sumir neðarr;

...she thought she was in her garden, and that she took a thorn out of her smock; and as she held it, it grew so that it became a great shoot, so that one end struck into the ground and was straightway rooted, while the other end towered high in the air. Thereupon it seemed to her that the tree was so large that she could hardly see over it, and it was marvellously thick. The lowest part of the tree was red as blood, but the body of it was bright green, and up toward the branches it was snow-white. The

limar trésins váru svá miklar, at henni þóttu dreifask um allan Nóreg ok enn víðara.

limbs were many and great, some above and some below. The branches of the tree were so big that they seemed to her to spread out over all Norway, and even further.

Saga Hálfdanar Svarta, p. 39. Hálfdan, king of Norway, once had the following dream:

...honum sýndisk, at hann væri allra manna bezt hærðr ok var hár hans alt í lokkum, sumir síðir til jarðar, sumir í miðjan legg, sumir á kné, sumir í mjöðm, sumir miðja síðu, sumir á háls, en sumir ekki meir en sprotnir upp ór hausi sem knýflar, en á lokkum hans var hvers kyns litr, en einn lokkr sigraði alla með fegrð ok ljósleik ok mikilleik.

...he thought he had the most beautiful hair of anyone, and that it was all in locks, some reaching to the ground, some to the middle of the leg, some to the knee, some to the hip, some to the middle of the side, some to the neck, and some not more than grown out on the scalp in short tufts; every colour was included in his hair, but one lock surpassed all the others in beauty and brightness, length and thickness.

Saga Óláfs Konungs Tryggvasonar, pp. 140–2. A thrall of Earl Hákon, named Karkr, had these three dreams before he murdered the earl:

i

...maðr svartr ok illiligr fór hjá hellinum ok hræddisk hann þat, at hann myndi inn ganga, en sá maðr sagði honum, at Ulli var dauðr.

...a black and hideous man passed by the cave; he (Karkr) was afraid that he would come in. The man told him that Ulli was dead.

ii

...hann sá þá inn sama mann fara ofan aptr ok bað þá segja jarli, at þá váru lokin sund öll.

...he saw the same man come back again and he told him to tell the earl that all the channels were then closed.

iii

...ek var nú á Hlöðum ok lagði Óláfr Tryggvason gullmen á háls mér.

...I was at Hlaðir and Óláfr Tryggvason laid a gold necklace about my neck.

KD

7

Saga ins helga Óláfs Konungs, p. 377. Once, after King Óláfr had lain awake in bed a long time thinking over his plans, he dreamed as follows:

Hann sá mann standa fyrir rekkjunni mikinn ok vegligan ok hafði klæðnað dýrligan; bauð konungi þat helzt í hug, at þar myndi vera kominn Óláfr Tryggvason. Sá maðr mælti til hans: 'Ertu mjök hugsjúkr um ráðaætlan þína, hvert ráð þú skalt upp taka? Þat þykki mér undarligt, er þú velkir þat fyrir þér, svá þat, ef þú ætlask þat fyrir at leggja niðr konungstígn þá, er guð hefir gefit þér; slíkt it sama sú ætlan, at vera hér ok þiggja ríki af útlendum konungum ok þér ókunnum; farðu heldr aptr til ríkis þíns, er þú hefir at erfðum tekit ok ráðit lengi fyrir með þeim styrk, er guð gaf þér, ok lát eigi undirmenn þína hræða þik; þat er konungs frami at sigrask á óvinum sínum, en vegligr dauði, at falla í orrostu með liði sínu; eða efar þú nökkut um þat, at þú hafir rétt at mæla í yðarri deilu? Eigi skaltu þat gera, at dylja sjálfan þik sannenda; fyrir því máttu djarfliga sœkja til landzins, at guð mun þér bera vitni, at þat er þín eiga'. En er konungr vaknaði, þá þóttisk hann sjá svip mannzins, er brot gekk.

He saw standing by the bed a large and noble man dressed in glorious clothing; the king was most inclined to think that it was Óláfr Tryggvason who had come. The man said to him: 'Are you very sick at heart as to what plan you should take up? It seems remarkable to me that you should hesitate, as if you intended to lay down the royal prerogative which God has given you; it is the same with regard to that other plan, to stay here and accept dominion from a king (kings) foreign and unknown; go back, rather, to your kingdom which you have received by inheritance and ruled before a long time with such strength as God gave you, and do not let your subordinates frighten you. It is a king's fame to gain the victory over his enemies, and a glorious death to fall in battle with one's following; or do you have any doubt that you have right on your side? You shall not hide the truth from yourself. For this reason you may lay claim to the land boldly, that God will bear you witness that it is your own'. When the king wakened he thought he saw a fleeting glimpse of the man as he went away.

Saga Haraldz Konungs Harðráða, pp. 500–1. Before they sailed for England, two of King Haraldr Harðráði's men had the following dreams:

i

...Gyrðr...þóttisk þar vera staddr á konungsskipinu ok sá

...Gyrðr...thought he was there on the king's ship and that he

upp á eyna, hvar tröllkona mikil
stóð ok hafði skálm í hendi, en í
annarri hendi trog; hann þóttisk
ok sjá yfir öll skip þeira, at
honum þótti fugl sitja á hverjum
skipstafni, þat váru alt ernir ok
hrafnar; tröllkonan kvað:

'Víst es, at allvaldr (austan)
eggjar vestr at leggja
mót við marga knútu
(minn snúðr es þat) prúða;
kná valþiðurr velja
(veit œrna sér beitu)
steik af stillis haukum
stafns; fylgik því (jafnan).'

looked up on to the island where
a great troll woman stood; she
had a short sword in one hand
and a trough in the other; he
thought he saw over all their ships,
and it seemed to him that a bird
was perched on every stern, and
that they were all eagles and
ravens. The troll woman said:

'It is certain that the king
from the east is bent upon
meeting many a glorious bone
in the west. It is profitable for
me; the raven will get food
from the king's ships; it knows
that there is abundant food for
it there; I always support this.'

ii

Þórðr...þóttisk sjá flota Haraldz
konungs fara at landi; þóttisk
vita, at þat var England; hann sá
á landinu fylking mikla, ok þótti
sem hvárirtveggju bjoggisk til
orrostu ok höfðu merki mörg á
lopti, en fyrir liði landzmanna
reið tröllkona mikil ok sat á vargi,
ok hafði vargrinn mannz hræ í
munni, ok fell blóð um kjaptana;
en er hann hafði þann etit, þá
kastaði hon öðrum í munn honum
ok síðan hverjum at öðrum en
hann gleypði hvern; hon kvað:

'Skœð lætr skína rauðan
skjöld, es dregr at hjaldri;
brúðr sér Aurnis jóða
óför konungs görva;
sviptir sveiflannkjapta
svanni holdi manna;
ulfs munn litar innan
óðlöt kona blóði—
ok óðlöt kona blóði.'

Þórðr dreamed that he saw King
Haraldr's fleet sail toward land,
and he seemed to know that that
was England; he saw a great host
on the land, and it seemed to him
as if each of them was preparing
for battle and had many banners
flying; before the company of the
landsmen a great troll woman rode
on a wolf, and the wolf had in his
mouth the dead body of a man, and
blood fell from the jaws. When
he had eaten that one, she threw
another into his mouth, and so on
one after the other; he swallowed
each one. She said a verse:

'The troll woman lets the red
shield shine, now when it is
drawing up to battle. The
bride of giants sees the down-
fall of the king prepared; the
woman gashes the men's flesh
with her jaws; the furious
woman dyes the inside of the
wolf's mouth with blood—the
furious woman with blood.'

Saga Magnús-sona, p. 547. Before Haraldr *gilli* came to Norway, King Sigurðr Magnússon had this dream:

...'ek þóttumk hér á Jaðri vera úti staddr ok sá ek út í haf ok leit ek þar sorta mikinn ok var för í ok nálgaðisk hingat; þá sýndisk mér, sem þat væri mikit tré eitt, ok óðu limarnar uppi, en rœtrnar í sjá. En er tréit kom at landi, þá braut þat ok rak brot trésins víða um landit, bæði um meginland ok úteyjar, sker ok strandir; ok þá gaf mér sýn, svá at ek þóttumk sjá um allan Nóreg it ýtra með sjá ok sá ek í hverja vík, at rekin váru brot af þessu tré, ok váru flest smá, en sum stœrri.'

...'I thought I was outside here in Jaðarr; I looked out to sea and saw a great black cloud moving swiftly in this direction. At that it seemed to me as if it were a large tree, and that the branches reached above the water while the roots were in the sea. When the tree came to land it broke asunder and pieces drifted wide about the land, both about the mainland, and the outer islands, the skerries and the shores. Then sight was given to me and I thought I saw over all the coast of Norway, and I saw that fragments of the tree had been carried into every creek; most of them were small but some were larger.'

Saga Magnús-sona, p. 553. A Dane, who had broken a vow made to Saint Ólafr in return for his miraculous escape from heathen capture, had the following dream:

...sá hann meyjar iii ganga til sín, fríðar ok fagrbúnar, ok ortu orða á hann þegar ok börðu hann miklum ávítum, er hann skyldi svá djarfr gerask, at hlaupa frá þeim góða konungi, er honum hafði svá mikla miskunn veitt, fyrst er hann leysti hann ór járnum ok allri prísund, ok firrask þann ljúfa lávarð, er hann hafði á hönd gengit. Því næst vaknaði hann.

...he saw three young women, beautiful and well dressed, come to him. They spoke to him at once and reproached him much that he should be so bold as to run away from the good king who had shown him such mercy, first releasing him from irons, and then from prison, and that he should shun the dear Lord under whose protection he had gone. Then he awoke.

Hervarar Saga ok Heiðreks. (*Fas.* I, pp. 309–60.)

Fas. I, p. 313. The night before he returned home from Earl Bjartmarr, Angantýr had this dream:

'Ek þóttist vera staddr í Sámsey og brœðr mínir; þar fundum vér

'I thought I was at Sámsey, together with my brothers; we saw

marga fugla, ok drápum alla, er vér sám; ok síðan þótti mér, sem vér snerim annan veg á eyna, ok flugu móti oss ernir tveir, ok gekk ek móti öðrum, ok áttum vit hart viðrskifti saman; ok um síðir settumst vit niðr ok vórum til einkis fœrir. Enn annarr arinn átti við ellifu brœðr mína og vann alla þá.'

many birds there and we killed all that we saw. Then it seemed to me that we went to another part of the island, and that two eagles flew toward us; I went against one of them and we had hard dealings with one another; at last we collapsed and all our strength was gone from us. The other eagle fought with my eleven brothers and overcame them all.'

Hœnsa-þóris Saga.

P. 18. While his father's homestead was being burned, Hersteinn Blund-Ketilsson dreamed as follows:

'Mik dreymdi, at mer þótti, sem faðir minn gengi hér inn, ok loguðu um hann klæðin öll, ok allr þótti mér sem hann væri eldr einn.'

'I dreamed that my father walked in here, and all the clothes flamed about him, and it seemed to me that he was all one fire.'

Hrafnkels Saga Freysgoða.

Pp. 1–2. When Hrafnkell was fifteen, his father, Hallfreðr, had the following dream:

...maðr kom at honum ok mælti: 'Þar liggr þú, Hallfreðr, ok heldr óvarlegr; fær þú á braut bú þitt ok vestr yfir Lagarfljót; þar er heill þín öll'.

...a man came to him and said: 'You lie there, Hallfreðr, and are rather unwary; remove your household away west over Lagar-fljót; there is all your good fortune'.

Hrólfs Saga Gautrekssonar. (Fas. III, pp. 41–141.)

Fas. III, pp. 56–7. Before Hrólfr Gautreksson came to Sweden on the first (unsuccessful) wooing expedition, Queen Ingigerðr had the following dream:

'Úti var ek stödd, ok þóttumst ek litast um, enn því brá við, at sá um alla Svíþjóð, ok miklu víðara; ek sá upp til Gautlands, ok svá gerla at ek sá þaðan renna varga-flokk mikinn, ok hingat þótti mér

'I was outside, and I thought I looked about, and it seemed strange inasmuch as I saw over all Sweden, and much further. I saw up into Gautland, and so clearly that I could distinguish a

þeir stefna á Svíþjóð, enn fyrir vörgunum fór hit óarga dýr; þat var harla mikit; þar fór eftir hvítabjörn; þat var rauðkinnr; bæði þótti mér dýrin sléttfjölluð ok kyrleg, ok láta ógrimmlega, enn þat þótti mér með ólíkendum, hversu skjótt hingat bar dýrin, eða hversu gerla ek þóttumst þau sjá, ok eigi þótti mér færri saman enn sex tigir; ek þóttumst vita, at þau mundu hingat ætla til Uppsala; ek þóttist kalla á þik ok segja þér til ok í því vaknaða ek.'

great pack of wolves running thence, and I thought they were coming in the direction of Sweden. Before the wolves went a lion; he was very large. A white bear followed him which was red-cheeked. It seemed to me that the animals were smooth-coated and quiet, and behaved in a friendly way, but I thought it curious how quickly they approached, and how clearly I could see them; it did not seem that there were less than sixty together. I felt sure that they were coming here to Uppsala, and I thought I called you and told you about it, and at that I awoke.'

Fas. III, p. 70. The night on which Hrólfr and his companions came to Sweden on the second expedition, Queen Ingigerðr dreamed as follows:

'Ek þóttumst enn úti standa, ok var mér enn víðsýnt; ek sá til sjóvar, at hér vóru komin skip eigi allfá við land, enn af skipunum runnu margir vargar, enn fyrir vörgunum fór et óarga dýr; þar með fóru hvítabirnir tveir harðla miklir ok vænlegir; fóru þessi dýr öll jafnframt, enn öðrum megin fram hjá óargadýrinu hljóp fram göltr einn; hann var ekki svá mikill, sem hann var víglegr, svá at slíkan hefi ek engan séð; hann rótaði hverri hæð, ok lét sem hann mundi umsnúa, ok fram horfði hvert hár á honum; hann lét sem hann mundi á alt hlaupa, ok bíta þat er í nánd var. Nú þykjumst ek vita, at þar sem hit óarga dýr er, at þat er fylgja Hrólfs konungs, svá sem ek sá

'I thought I was standing outside, and that I again had a wide outlook. My sight reached to the sea and I saw that not a few ships had come to land here; many wolves ran from the ships, and before them a lion; two very big and fine white bears were with them. The wolves ran all abreast, but on one side, in front by the lion, sped a boar. He was not very large but he was so fierce that I have never seen anything like it. He rooted up every hill, acting as if he would turn it inside out, and every hair stood on end; he behaved as if he would rush at everything and bite whatever was near. Now I feel sure that, as regards the lion, it is the fetch of King Hrólfr just as I saw it before, though now it was much

hana fyrr, enn þó var hún nú miklu ófrýnlegri enn fyrr ok öll dýrin miklu grimmlegri, ok runnu þegar á land upp ok á leið til Uppsala.'

more angry-looking, and all the beasts much more fierce. They ran on land immediately, and along the road to Uppsala.'

Hrómundar Saga Greipssonar. (*Fas.* II, pp. 325–36.)

Fa.. II, pp. 335–6. One winter Blindr related the following dreams, prophetic of the revenge to be taken by Hrómundr Greipsson for the slaying of his brothers, to King Haddingr:

i

'Mér þótti vargr einn renna austan, hann beit yðr, konungr, ok veitti yðr áverka.'

'I thought I saw a wolf run from the east; he bit you, King, and gave you a wound.'

ii

Enn kvað Blindr sik dreymt hafa, at honum þótti margir haukar sitja í einu húsi—'ok þekti ek þar fálka þinn, herra; hann var allr fjaðralauss ok fiettr hamnum'.

Again Blindr said that he had dreamed that he thought many hawks were sitting in a house—'and I recognized your falcon among them, Lord; he was all featherless and flayed'.

iii

'Mörg svín sá ek renna sunnan at konungs höllu, rótuðu jörðinni upp með rananum.'

'I saw many swine running from the south towards the king's hall; they rooted up the ground with their snouts.'

iv

'Mér þótti einn ógurlegr hriki koma austan at; hann beit yðr stóra und.'

'It seemed to me that an awful giant came hither from the east; he bit you, giving you a great wound.'

v

...'mér þótti liggja um Svíaveldi grimmlegr ormr.'

...'I thought a fierce serpent was lying coiled about Sweden.'

vi

...'mér þótti koma af landi svört ský með klóm ok vængjum, ok flugu brott með þik, konungr.'

...'I dreamed that black clouds with claws and wings came from the land and flew away with you, King.'

vii

...'þá dreymdi mik enn, at ormr einn væri hjá Hagali karli; sá beit menn grimmlega; át hann bæði mik ok yðr upp ok alla konungs menn.'

...'then again I dreamed that a serpent was with the man Hagall. He bit people fiercely; he devoured both you and me and all the king's men.'

viii

'Hér næst dreymdi mik, at dreka hamr væri dreginn um konungs höll, ok hekk þar við lindi Hrómunds.'

'Next I dreamed that a dragon's skin had been drawn about the king's hall, and that Hrómundr's shield was hanging to it.'

ix

'Mér þótti járnhringr settr á minn háls.'

'I thought an iron ring was placed about my neck.'

Íslendingabók.

P. 8. Before the meeting of the Althing at which the calendar was reformed, Þorsteinn Surtr had the following dream:

...hann hygþisc vesa at lögbergi, þá es þar vas fiölment, oc vaca, en hann hugþi alla menn aþra sova, en síþan hugþisc hann sofna, en hann hugþi þá alla menn aþra vacna.

...he dreamed that he was at the Law-rock when the Thing was crowded; he was awake but thought everyone else asleep; afterwards he thought he fell asleep, and that all the other people awoke.

Jómsvíkinga Saga. (*Fms.* 11, pp. 1–176.)

Fms. 11, pp. 5–6. Before his marriage with Þyri, King Gormr had these three dreams prophetic of nine years of famine:

i

...hann þóttist úti staddr vera, ok sjá yfir allt ríke sitt, hann sá at sjórinn féll út frá landi svá lángt, at hann mátte hvergi auga yfir reka, ok svá mikil varð fjaran, at þurr voro öll eyjasundin ok firðir; en eptir þessi tíðendi sá hann, at eyxn 3 hvítir gingu upp or sænum, ok runno á land

...he dreamed that he was outside and was looking over all his kingdom. He saw that the sea had ebbed so far from land that his eye could not reach it, and that the tidal flats were so great that all the straits between the islands and the firths were dry. Next he saw that three white

upp, þar nær sem hann var, ok bito af allt gras at snöggu, þar er þeir komo at, ok eptir þat þá gingo þeir á braut.

oxen came from the sea and ran up on to the land close to where he was, and ate all the grass down to the ground wherever they went. After that they went away.

ii

Sá var annarr draumr, er þessom er mjök áþekkr, at honum þykkir enn sem 3 eyxn ginge upp or sænom, þeir voru rauðir at lit ok hyrndir mjök, þeir bito enn gras af jörðunne, jafnt sem enir fyrre, ok er þeir höfðu þar verit nokkverja hríð, þá gingu þeir enn aptr í sæinn.

The second dream, which was much like this, was that it again seemed to him that three oxen came up out of the sea. They were red and had large horns. They cropped the grass down to the ground as had the former ones; when they had been there for some time they went back into the sea.

iii

Enn dreymdi hann enn 3ja draum, ok var sá enn þessom líkr; enn þóttist konúngrinn sjá þrjá eyxn ganga upp or sjónum, þeir voru allir svartir at lit ok miklo mest hyrndir, ok voru enn nokkora hríð, ok fóru ena sömo leið í braut, ok gingo aptr í sjóinn; ok eptir þat þóttist hann heyra brest svá mikinn, at hann hugðe, at heyra munde um alla Danmörk, ok sá hann, at þat varð af sjófar- ganginom, er hann gekk at landino.

He dreamed yet a third dream, and this was again like the others. The king once more saw three oxen come up out of the sea. They were all black, and with much the largest horns; they stayed a while, and left in the same way, and went back into the sea. After that he heard a crash so great that he felt that it must be heard over all Denmark; he saw that it was made by the sea as it drove against the shore.

Jóns Saga hins Helga. (*Bks.* I, pp. 215–60.)

Bks. I, p. 246. One night Jón, bishop of Hólar, had the following dream:

Hann þóttist vera á bæn sinni fyrir einum miklum róðukrossi; ok því næst þótti honum líknesit á krossinum hneigjast at sér, ok mæla nokkur orð í eyru sér, ok vitum vér eigi hver þau vóru.

He thought he was at his prayers before a great crucifix, and all at once it seemed to him that the figure on the cross leaned toward him, and whispered some words into his ear; we do not know what they were.

Knytlínga Saga. (Fms. 11, pp. 179–402.)

Fms. 11, p. 371. Before his victory over King Sveinn, King Valdimarr Knútsson had this dream:

...hann þóttist sjá enn helga Knut lávarð föður sinn, ok mælti við hann: 'Hér liggr þú, son minn!' sagði hann, 'ok ert mjök óttafullr um skipti ykkar Sveins konúngs, hvern veg fara munu; ver hraustr enn,' sagði hann, 'þvíat þú hefir góð málefni í ykkrum deilum; hygg at nú vandliga, hvat ek segi þér, son minn! þvíat þetta er ekki fals, er fyrir þik ber: þá er þú vaknar, muntu sjá hvar hrafn einn flýgr, ok þat skaltu vandliga hugsa, hvar hann sezt, þvíat þar skaltu skipa fylkíng þína, sem hrafninn nemr stað, ok mun guð þér sigr gefa'. Eptir þetta vaknar Valdimarr konúngr.

...he dreamed that he saw his father, the sainted Knut lávarð, who spoke to him thus: 'Here you lie, my son,' said he, 'and are much troubled about what the outcome of your dealings with Sveinn is to be; be of good courage,' said he, 'for you have right on your side; pay careful attention to what I tell you, my son, because it is not false: when you wake you will see a raven fly, and you must notice exactly where it lights, for you must draw up your following where it settles, and then God will give you the victory'. After that King Valdimarr awoke.

Landnámabók (Hauksbók).

P. 14. A byre-maid of Halldórr Illugason, who was in the habit of wiping her feet on the mound which marked the grave of Ásólfr Alskik, once dreamed as follows:

...hana dreymdi at Ásólfr avitadi hana vm þat er hun þerdi fætr sinasaurga a hvsi hans. 'Enn þa munu vit satt,' segir hann, 'ef þu seger Halldóri draum þinn.'

...she dreamed that Ásólfr rebuked her for drying her feet of their soiling on his house. 'But we shall be reconciled', said he, 'if you tell your dream to Halldórr.'

Some time later a monk living in the neighbourhood had this dream:

...dreymdi at Ásólfr mællti vid hann: 'Sendtu hyskarl þinn til Halldórs at Hólmi ok kaup at hanum þvfu þa er a fiosgotu er ok gef vid mork silfrs'.

...he dreamed that Ásólfr said to him: 'Send your servant to Halldórr at Hólmr and buy the mound which is by the byrepath, and pay for it with a mark of silver'.

The night after the monk had bought the mound, Halldórr had this dream:

...Ásólfr kom at hanum ok kuezt bædi augu mvndv sprengia or hausi hanum nema hann keypti bein hans sliku verdi sem hann selldi.

...Ásólfr came to him and said that both his eyes would burst out of his head unless he bought his bones for the same price as he sold them.

Pp. 24–5. When Ásmundr Atlason died, a thrall of his took his own life to follow him and was buried in the same howe:

...litlv siðar dreymði Þorv at Asmvndr sagði ser mefn at Þrælnvm...visa þersi var heyrð i havg hans. 'Ein bygi ek stoð steina stafnrvm atals rafni erað of þegn a þilivm þrong by ek a mar ranga rvm er boðvitrvm betra brimdyri kna ek styra lifa mvn þat með lofðvm lengr en illt of gengi.'

...a little later Þóra (Ásmundr's wife) dreamed that Ásmundr said that the thrall was a trouble to him....This verse was heard in his howe. 'I inhabit the prow-room of the ship in the howe alone; there is no crowding about the man on the deck; I live in the ship; ample room is better for the man skilled in battle, how-ever, than a poor following; that following will always be re-membered by people. I command the ship.'

P. 78. Þorgeirr of Hvínverjadalr once discovered the identity of some strangers who had visited him thus:

...dreymdi at kona kvæmi at hanvm ok segði hanvm hverir gestir með hanvm hofðv verit.

...he dreamed that a woman came to him and told him what guests had been with him.

P. 90. Hrafnkell Hrafnsson had the following dream before a landslip overwhelmed the spot where he had fallen asleep while on a journey:

...maðr kom at hanvm ok bað hann vpp standa ok fara brott sem skiotaz.

...a man came to him and told him to get up and go away as quickly as he could.

P. 101. Björn Molda-Gnúpsson of Grindavík once had the following dream:

...bergbvi kvemi at hanvm ok byði at gera felag við hann en

...a giant (cliff-dweller) came to him and offered to go into partner-

108   APPENDIX
body

hann iatti. þa kom hafr til geita
hans litlv siðar. því var hann
Hafr-Björnn kallaðr, hann gerðiz
bœði rikr ok storavðigr. þat sa
vfresk kona at allar landvettir
fylgðv Hafrbirnni þa er hann fór
til þings enn Þorsteini ok Þorði
brœðrvm hans þa er þeir fisktv.

ship with him; he accepted. A
little later a buck came to his
goats. For this reason he was
called Hafr-Björn. He became
powerful and very rich, and a
woman gifted with second sight
said that the guardian spirits of
the country-side accompanied
Hafr-Björn when he went to the
Thing, and were with Þorsteinn
and Þórðr, his brothers, when
they went fishing.

Laxdæla Saga.

P. 85. After killing his remarkable ox, Óláfr Pái had the following dream:

...kona kom at honum; sú var
mikil ok reiðuleg. Hon tók til
orða: 'Er þér svefns?' Hann
kvaðst vaka. Konan mælti: 'Þér
er svefns, en þó mun fyrir hitt
ganga. Son minn hefir þú drepa
látit ok koma ógervilegan mér
til handa, ok fyrir þá sök skaltu
eiga at sjá þinn son alblóðgan af
mínu tilstilli; skal ek ok þann til
velja, er ek veit, at þér er ófalastr'.
Síðan hvarf hon á brott. Óláfr
vaknaði ok þóttist sjá svip konunnar.

...a woman came to him; she
was large and angry-looking. She
began to speak: 'Are you dreaming?' He said he was awake.
The woman said: 'You are
dreaming, but, nevertheless, it
may go for the same thing. You
have had my son killed and have
let him come into my hands in a
wretched condition. On that account you shall see your son all
covered with blood by my
agency; and I shall pick out the
one whom I know it is hardest
for you to lose'. After that she
turned away. Óláfr awoke and
thought he saw a fleeting glimpse
of the woman.

Pp. 88–90. During the winter previous to her first marriage (with
Þorvaldr Halldórsson) Guðrún had the following four dreams
prophetic of her four marriages:

i

'Úti þóttumst ek vera stödd við
lœk nökkurn, ok hafða ek krók-
fald á höfði ok þótti mér illa
sama, ok var ek fúsari at breyta

'I thought I was by a brook, and
I had on head-gear which I felt
was unbecoming. I wanted to
change it, but many said that I

faldinum, en margir töldu um, at ek skylda þat eigi gera. En ek hlýdda ekki á þat, ok greip ek af höfði mér faldinn ok kastaða ek út á lœkinn.'

should not do so. I did not listen to that, and tore the hood off my head and threw it into the brook.'

ii

'Þat var upphaf at öðrum draum, at ek þóttumst vera stödd hjá vatni einu; svá þótti mér, sem kominn væri silfrhringr á hönd mér, ok þóttumst ek eiga ok einkarvel sama. Þótti mér þat vera allmikil gersemi ok ætlaða ek lengi at eiga, ok er mér váru minstar vánir, þá rendi hringrinn af hendi mér ok á vatnit, ok sá ek hann aldri síðan. Þótti mér sá skaði miklu meiri, en ek mætta at glíkendum ráða, þótt ek hefða einum grip týnt. Síðan vaknaða ek.'

'At the beginning of the second dream I seemed to be by a certain lake; I thought I had a silver ring on my arm, and it seemed that I owned it, and that it became me exceedingly well. I thought it was a great treasure and meant to keep it a long time. But when I was least expecting it, the ring slipped off my arm, and into the water, and I saw nothing more of it afterwards. The loss seemed to me much greater than I should be likely to feel, though a costly thing were gone. After that I awoke.'

iii

'Sá er enn þriði draumr minn, at ek þóttumst hafa gullhring á hendi ok þóttumst ek eiga hringinn, ok þótti mér bœttr skaðinn; kom mér þat í hug, at ek munda þessa hrings lengr njóta en ens fyrra; en eigi þótti mér sjá gripr því betri, sem gull er dýrra en silfr. Síðan þóttumst ek falla ok vilja styðja mik með hendinni, en gullhringrinn mœtti steini nökkurum ok stökk í tvá hluti, ok þótti mér dreyra ór hlutunum. Þat þótti mér líkara harmi en skaða, er ek þóttumst þá bera eftir; kom mér þá i hug, at brestr hafði verit á hringnum, ok þá er ek hugða at brotunum eftir, þá þóttumst ek sjá fleiri brestina á,

'This is my third dream; I thought I had a gold ring on my arm, and that my loss was compensated for; it came into my head that I should enjoy this ring longer than the former one; but I did not think that treasure as much better than the one (I had) before as gold is more precious than silver. Then I thought I fell, and I wanted to steady myself with my hand, but the gold ring struck against some stone and sprang apart in two pieces, and it seemed to bleed out of the fragments. I thought it was more like grief than loss which I felt after that; it came into my mind that there had been flaws in the ring,

ok þótti mér þó sem heill mundi, ef ek hefða betr til gætt.'

and when I looked at the pieces I thought I saw several flaws in it. Nevertheless, I felt that it might have been whole if I had taken better care of it.'

iv

'Sá er enn fjórði draumr minn, at ek þóttumst hafa hjálm á höfði af gulli, ok var settr mjök gimsteinum. Ek þóttumst eiga þá gersemi; en þat þótti mér helzt at, at hann var nökkurs til þungr; því at ek fekk varla valdit, ok bar ek halt höfuðit, ok gaf ek þó hjálminum enga sök á því, ok ætlaða ekki at lóga honum, en þó steyptist hann af höfði mér ok út á Hvammsfjörð.'

'This is my fourth dream; I thought I had a helmet of gold on my head, and it was much set with precious stones. I thought I owned that treasure. But it rather seemed to me that it was somewhat too heavy, because I could hardly carry it, and held my head on one side: nevertheless, I gave the helmet no blame on this account, and did not intend to part with it. However, it tumbled off my head and out into Hvammfirth.'

Pp. 153–4. The night before Kjartan was attacked by the sons of Ósvifr in Hafragil, Án the Black dreamed as follows:

'Kona kom at mér, óþekkileg, ok kipti mér á stokk fram. Hon hafði í hendi skálm ok trog í annarri; hon setti fyrir brjóst mér skálmina ok reist á mér kviðinn allan ok tók á brott innyflin ok lét koma í staðinn hrís; eftir þat gekk hon út.'

'A woman came to me, repulsive in appearance, and snatched me to the edge of the bed. She had in one hand a short sword and in the other a trough; she set the sword against my breast, and cut me all open. She took out my entrails, and put brush-wood in their place. After that she went out.'

P. 161. While lying in a swoon, as a result of wounds he received while helping Kjartan against the sons of Ósvifr at Hafragil, Án the Black had the following vision (cf. pp. 153–4 above):

'dreymdi mik en sama kona ok fyrr, ok þótti mér hon nú taka hrísit ór maganum, en lét koma innyflin í staðinn, ok varð mér gott við þat skifti.'

'I dreamed of the same woman as before, and I thought she took the brush-wood out of my stomach and instead put in my entrails, and the change seemed good to me.'

P. 226. Two years or so before he was drowned off Bjarnarey, Þorkell Eyjólfsson once dreamed:

'Þat dreymdi mik at ek þóttumst eiga skegg svá mikit, at tœki um allan Breiðafjörð.'

'I dreamed that I had such a big beard that it reached over all Broadfirth.'

P. 236. During the latter years of Guðrún's life, when she had become very devout, her granddaughter, Herdís, dreamed:

...at kona kœmi at henni; sú var í vefjarskikkju ok faldin höfuðdúki; ekki sýndist henni konan svipleg. Hon tók til orða: 'Seg þú þat ömmu þinni, at mér hugnar illa við hana, því at hon bröltir allar nætr á mér ok fellir á mik dropa svá heita, at ek brenn af öll. En því segi ek þér til þessa, at mér líkar til þín nökkuru betr, en þó svífr enn nökkut kynlegt yfir þik; en þó munda ek við þik semja, ef mér þœtti eigi meiri bóta vant, þar sem Guðrún er'.

...that a woman came to her; she was in a woven cloak and was wearing a folded head-kerchief. She did not seem pleasant. She began to speak: 'Tell your grandmother that I am displeased with her because she tumbles about on me every night, and sheds such hot drops on me that I burn all over from them. But I tell you about this because I like you somewhat better, although something strange hovers about you too; nevertheless, I could treat with you if I did not think there was so much more the matter with Guðrún'.

Ljósvetninga Saga.

Pp. 96–7. Eyjólfr Guðmundarson once had the following dream before becoming involved in certain difficulties:

'Ek þóttumst ríða norðr háls, ok sá ek nautaflokk koma í mót mér; þar var í oxi einn mikill, rauðr; hann vildi illa við mik gera; þar var ok graðungr mannýgr ok margt smáneyti. Þá kom yfir mik þoka mikil ok sá ek eigi nautin.'

'I thought I was riding north of the ridge, and saw a herd of cattle coming toward me; in it was a great red ox, and he wanted to deal roughly with me; there was also a vicious bull and many calves. Next, a thick mist came over me so that I could not see the herd.'

Njáls Saga.

P. 54. When things were going badly for his half-brother, Hrútr, Höskuldr Dala-Kollsson had the following dream:

...'ek þóttumst sjá bjarndýri mikit ganga út ór húsunum—ok vissa ek at eigi fanst þessa dýrs maki—ok fylgdu því húnar tveir, ok vildu þeir vel dýrinu. Þat stefndi til Hrútsstaða ok gekk þar inn í húsin. Síðan vaknaði ek.'

...'I thought I saw a great bear go out of the house, and I knew that the match for this beast was not to be found, and two cubs followed it, and wished the bear well. He made for Hrútsstaðir, and went into the house there. Then I awoke.'

P. 145. Just before the attack on Gunnarr and Hjörtr made by Starkaðr of Því-hyrningi and Egill Kollsson at Rangánes, Gunnarr had this dream:

...'ek þóttumst ríða fram hjá Knafahólum. Þar þóttumst ek sjá varga mjök marga, ok sóttu þeir allir at mér, enn ek snera undan fram at Rangá. Þá þótti mér þeir sækja at öllum megin, enn ek vörðumst. Ek skaut alla þá, er fremstir váru þar til er þeir gengu svá at mér, at ek mátta eigi boganum við koma. Tók ek þá sverðit ok vá ek með annarri hendi, enn lagða með atgeirinum annarri hendi. Hlífða ek mér þá ekki, ok þóttumst ek þá eigi vita, hvat mér hlífði. Drap ek þá marga vargana ok þú með mér, Kolskeggr. Enn Hjört þótti mér þeir hafa undir ok slíta á honum brjóstit ok hafði einn hjartat í munni sér. Enn ek þóttumst verða svá reiðr, at ek hjó varginn í sundr fyrir aftan bóguna, ok eftir þat þóttu mér stökkva vargarnir.'

...'I thought I was riding on by Knafahólar. I seemed to see very many wolves, and they all attacked me, but I retreated toward Rang river. Then I thought they came upon me from all sides, but I defended myself. I shot all those which were foremost, until they made at me so that I might not use my bow. Then I took my sword and fenced with it in one hand, and thrust with my halberd with the other. I did not protect myself then, and I did not know what shielded me. Thereupon I killed many of the wolves, and you, Kolskeggr, did likewise; but it seemed that they had Hjörtr down and were tearing at his breast, and that one had his heart in its mouth. I thought that I became so furiously angry that I hewed the wolf asunder just behind the withers; after that the wolves fled.'

Pp. 326–7. Some time after the 'burning-in' of Njáll and his household, Flosi, the leader of the burners, had this dream:

'Mik dreymdi þat, at ek þóttumst staddr at Lómagnúpi ok ganga út ok sjá upp til gnúpsins. Ok opnaðist hann. Ok gekk maðr út ór gnúpinum ok var í geitheðni ok hafði járnstaf í hendi. Hann fór kallandi ok kallaði á menn mína—suma fyrr enn suma síðar—ok nemndi þá á namn. Hann kallaði fyrstan Grím hinn rauða frænda minn ok Árna Kolsson. Þa þótti mér undarlega við bregða. Mér þótti hann þá kalla Eyjólf Bölverksson ok Ljót son Halls af Síðu ok nakkvara sex menn. Þá þagði hann stund nakkvara. Síðan kallaði hann fimm menn af váru liði, ok váru þar Sigfússynir bræðr þínir. Þá kallaði hann aðra fimm menn ok var þar Lambi ok Móðúlfr ok Glúmr. Þá kallaði hann þrjá menn. Síðast kallaði hann Gunnar Lambason ok Kol Þorsteinsson. Eftir þat gekk hann at mér. Ek spurða hann tíðenda. Hann lézt kunna at segja tíðendin. Þa spurða ek hann at namni. Enn hann nemndist Járngrímr. Ek spurða, hvert hann skyldi fara. Hann kvaðst fara skyldu til alþingis. "Hvat skalt þú þar gera?" sagða ek. Hann svaraði: "Fyrst skal ek ryðja kviðu, enn þá dóma, enn þá vígvöll fyrir vegöndum". Síðan kvað hann þetta:

"Höggorma mun hefjask
herði-Þundr á landi;
séa munu menn á moldu

'I dreamed that I was at Lómagnúpr, and went out and looked up at the peak. At that it opened. A man came out of the peak, and was wearing a goatskin jacket and carrying an iron staff in his hand. He went along calling and called on my men—some before and some after—and named them by name. First he called Grímr the Red, my kinsman, and Árni Kolsson. It seemed to me uncanny. Then I thought he called Eyjólfr Bölverksson, and Ljótr, son of Hallr of Síða, and some six others. Then he was quiet awhile. Afterwards he called five men of our band, and the sons of Sigfúss, your brothers, were among them. Then he called another group of five and among them were Lambi and Móðúlfr and Glúmr. Next he called three men. Last he called Gunnarr Lambason and Kolr Þorsteinsson. Then he came toward me. I asked him the news and he admitted he had tidings to tell. Thereupon I asked him his name; he gave his name as Járngrímr (Irongrim). I asked where he was going. He said he was going to the Althing. "What are you going to do there?" I asked. He answered, "First I shall challenge the jury, and then I shall challenge the courts, and then I shall clear the battlefield for fighting". Then he said this:

"A warrior will appear in the land; one will see many heads on the ground. The fight is

marga heila borgir;
nú vex blára brodda
beystisullr í fjöllum;
koma mun sumra seggja
sveita-dögg á leggi."
Hann laust niðr stafnum, ok varð
brestr mikill. Gekk hann þá inn
í fjallit. En mér bauð ótta.'

growing now in the mountains;
blood will stream down some
men's legs."

He struck down the staff, and
there was a great crash. After
that he went into the mountain.
I still felt afraid.'

Reykdæla Saga.

P. 67. The night after he had replaced the sword, Skefils-
nautr, in the tomb of its dead owner, Þorkell Geirason had this
dream:

...bar Þorkatli Skefil í drauma,
ok kvað Þorkel munu vera góðan
dreng ok þakkaði honum, hvé
hann hafði drengilega dugat, ok
svá sverðit haft. 'Enn ef þú
hefðir eigi viljat, at aftr hefði verit
berit sverðit, þá myndir þú hafa
goldit þess í nökkuru. Enn nú
mun fara með okkr annan veg,
því at nú skal hvárrgi illa hafa,
svá vel sem þér hefir farit, ok vil
ek gefa þér sverðit, því at ek þarf
þat nú ekki, enn þú ert svá vaskr
maðr, at ek ann þér allvel at
njóta.' Ok nú vaknar Þorkell, ok
var þar komit sverðit.

...Skefill appeared to Þorkell in
his dreams; he said Þorkell must
be a fine fellow, and thanked him
for the brave way in which he had
acted, and for having wielded the
sword so well. 'But if you had
not wanted to have it brought
back you would have paid for it
somehow. Now it will go another
way between us, for neither of us
shall suffer evil, since you have
been so honourable. I will give
you the sword, because I do not
need it any more, and you are a
valiant man and it pleases me that
you should have it.' When
Þorkell woke the sword was
there.

Saga Guðmundar Arasonar, Viðbætir. (Bks. 1, pp. 560–618.)

Bks. 1, p. 590. The night after he had asked the Virgin
Mary to bless his voyage to Iceland, Bishop Guðmundr had this
dream:

...sýndist honum í svefni sæl
María guðs móðir, ok var blíð
við hann, ok sagði honum marga
hluti, þá er hann vissi eigi áðr,
bæði af Íslandi ok anna(rs) staðar.

...the blessed Mary, Mother of
God, appeared to him in his sleep
and was friendly to him, and told
him many things he did not
know before, both of Iceland and
elsewhere.

Saga Ólafs Konúngs Tryggvasonar. (*Fms.* 1 and 2.)

Fms. 2, p. 162. A tenth-century Christian convert in Norway had the following dream before his fanatical brother came home to desecrate the family temple to Þórr:

...um nóttina, áðr Finnr kom, dreymdi Svein bróður hans Þórr heldr úfrýnligr ok daprligr; hann mælti: 'Hér kemr nú at því með okkr, sem mælt er, at fyrnist vinskapr sem fundir, ok þó at þat sé svá sem er, þá vildi ek biðja þik eins lutar, at þú flyttir mik braut af húsi mínu til skógar, því at Finnr bróðir þinn mun heim koma, ok hygg ek ekki gott til hans kvámu'. Sveinn svarar: 'Því hefir ek heitit konúngi, at skipta mér engu af við þik, ok þat mun ek halda; þikkir mér þú ok guðleysi, ef þú hefir eigi mátt til at forða þér við háska, eðr flytja þik sjálfr hvert er þú vill'. Hvarf Þórr í braut hrygðarfullr ok harms, en Sveinn vaknaði.

...the night before Finnr arrived, Sveinn, his brother, dreamed that Þórr came to him. He was frowning much and sad; he said: 'Now it has come to this between us, that, as the saying goes, friendship grows colder as meetings grow fewer, but, though conditions are as they are, I beg one thing of you, that you take me from my house into the woods, because Finnr, your brother, is coming home, and I anticipate nothing good from his coming'. Sveinn answered: 'I have promised the king to have no dealings with you, and I shall keep my word; it seems to me, too, that you are ungodlike if you have not power to safeguard yourself against peril, or move wherever you wish'. Þórr disappeared, troubled and full of grief. Sveinn awoke.

Sögubrot af Fornkonungum. (*Fas.* 1, pp. 285–305.)

Fas. 1, p. 288. King Hrœrekr once had the following dream:

'Mik dreymdi, at ek væra staddr nær skógi nokkurum, ok hjá völlr sléttr ok fagr, ok þar sá ek einn hjört standa á vellinum; þá rann ór skóginum einn hlébarðr, ok þótti mér fax hans sem gull, ok hjörtrinn stakk hornunum undir bóg dýrinu, enn þat fell dautt niðr; þar næst sá ek, hvar flaug flugdreki mikill, ok kom þar, sem hjörtrinn var, ok greip

'I dreamed that I was close to a wood, and near a beautiful level meadow on which I saw a stag standing. Then a leopard ran out of the wood and it seemed to me that his mane was like gold; the stag pierced him with his horns under the shoulder so that he fell dead; next I saw a great winged dragon flying, and it came to where the stag was, and straight-

þegar í klœr sér, ok sleit allan í sundr; þá sa ek bjarndýr eitt, ok fylgdi húnn ungr, ok vildi drekinn taka hann, enn beran varði, ok vaknaða ek þá.'

way seized him in its talons, and tore him all to pieces. Then a mother bear appeared with a cub, and the dragon wanted to snatch the cub but the bear defended it. At that I awoke.'

Fas. I, pp. 291–2. One night, when King Ívarr was sleeping in the castle of the poop of his warship, he had this dream:

...honum þótti sem dreki mikill flygi utan af hafinu, ok þótti litr hans sem gull eitt, ok sindra af honum upp á himininn, sem síur flygi ór afli, ok lýsir á öll lönd en næstu af honum; ok þar eftir fljúga allir fuglar þeir, sem honum þóttu vera á norðrlöndum; ok þá sá hann í annan stað, at dregr upp ský mikit af landnorðri, ok sér, at þar fylgir svá mikit regn ok hvassviðri, at honum þótti, sem allir skógar ok alt land flyti í vatni því, sem ofan rigndi; þar fylgdu reiðar ok eldingar. Ok er sá enn mikli dreki fló af sænum á landit, kom móti honum regnit ok illviðrit, ok svá mikit myrkr, at því næst sá hann eigi drekann né fuglana, enn heyrði þó gný mikinn af reiðunum ok af illviðrinu, ok gekk alt svá suðr ok vestr um landit, ok svá víða sem hans ríki var; ok þá þóttist hann sjá þar til, sem skipin vóru, at öll vóru orðin at hvölum einum, ok renna út í haf, ok síðan vaknar hann.

...he thought that a great dragon was flying in from the sea, and it seemed to him that its colour was as of gold; light sparkled from it up against the sky like the fiery particles from the hearth of a forge, and all the lands about were illuminated; and in its wake flew all the birds he believed to be in the Northlands. Then he saw that a great cloud was coming up from the north-east from another direction, and that so much rain and such fierce gales accompanied it that all the woods and land seemed to be flooded with the rain. With this there was thunder and lightning. And when the great dragon flew from the sea to the land, the rain and gales came toward him, together with such thick darkness that all at once he could see neither the dragon nor the birds, but heard, nevertheless, the mighty crash of the thunder and lightning; the storm went south and west about the land as far as his dominion reached. Then he thought he looked at the place where the ships were, and they had all turned into as many whales, and were rushing out to sea. Thereupon he awoke.

Interpretation.

...ok hann lét kalla til sín Hörð fóstra sínn, ok segir honum drauminn, ok bað hann ráða. Hörðr kveðst vera svá gamlaðr, at hann kvaðst ekki kunna at skynja drauma; hann stóð í bjargi fyrir ofan bryggjusporð; enn konungr lá í lyftingu ok sprettir langskarir, er þeir rœddust við. Konunginum var óskaplétt, ok mælti: 'Gakk á skip, Hörðr, ok ráð draum minn'. Hörðr segist eigi munu út ganga; 'ok þarf eigi at ráða draum þinn; sjálfr máttu víta, hvat hann er, ok meiri ván, at skamt líði héðan, áðr skipast munu ríki í Svíþjóð ok Danmörk, ok er nú kominn á þik helgráðr, er þú hygst öll ríki munu undir þik leggja, enn þú veizt eigi, at hitt mun fram koma, at þú munt vera dauðr, enn ovínir þínir munu fá ríkit'.

...he called his foster-father to him, told him his dream and asked him to interpret it. Hörðr answered that he was so very old that he could not interpret dreams. He stood on a crag above the head of the pier, but the king lay in the poop-castle and was loosening the lower hem of the tent as they talked. The king was moody and said: 'Come on to the ship, Hörðr, and read my dream'. Hörðr answered that he would not come out to him—'and it is not necessary to interpret your dream; you must know yourself what it means, and it is more to be expected that it will be but a short time before there will be a change of rule in Sweden and Denmark. Even now the death-greed has come upon you in that you think to subdue to yourself all dominion, but you do not know that it is to come to pass that you meet your death, and that your enemies take over your sovereignty'.

Fulfilment.

Hörðr (Óðinn) is really the arbiter of King Ívarr's destiny here, since he is drowned as the result of an attack on his supposed foster-father, directly provoked by the latter.

Sögubrot um Jón Arason. (*Bks.* II, pp. 421–507.)

Bks. II, pp. 421–2. Shortly before she was married, the mother of Jón, bishop of Hólar, had this dream:

...hafi hún þókzt verða barns hafandi og gjörast þúnguð, og ala orm eða naður; þá þóttist

...she thought she was with child, and became heavy and brought forth a serpent or an

hún fara höndum um hann, sem
barn væri, og leggja hann í
kjöltu sér, því engi stóð henni
ógn af honum; þótti henni
glerlitur vera á honum, og sléttur
á bakið að finna, og mjúkur og háll;
og í drauminum þá var sem hún
heyrði einhvern segja: 'Þessum
ormi er fyrirhugað og búið hreysi
undir innra kórnum í dómkirk-
junni á Hólum'. Þá er hún hafði
heyrt þetta vaknaði hún.

adder. It seemed to her that she
put her arms about it, and laid
it in her lap, for she was not
afraid of it. She thought that it
was the colour of glass, with
spots on its back, and that it was
soft and slippery. In the dream
it was as if she heard someone
say: 'The destiny of this serpent
is fixed, and a den is prepared for
it under the inner choir in the
Cathedral at Hólar'. When she
had heard this, she awoke.

Bks. II, p. 452. Not long before his death, Bishop Jón had
this dream:

...að hann legði glófa sinn á
altarið í Skálholts kirkju og
skildi þar eptir.

...that he had laid his glove on
the altar in the church at Skálholt,
and left it there.

Sturlunga Saga.

Vol. I, p. 106. Before he was drowned in Ísafjörðr, Páll
Þórðarson had this dream:

...dræmdi Pal Þorðarson hann
þottiz vera i skyckðum linkyrtli.

...Páll Þórðarson dreamed that
he was dressed in a shining linen
kirtle.

Vol. I, pp. 258–9. Before Guðmundr Arason was made bishop,
his uncle, Þorvarðr Þorgeirsson, related the following dream to
him:

'Mik dreymdi, at ek skylldi ganga
inn i hus micit oc hatt, enn ek
hefdi ecki iafn-mikit sed, oc sva
miclar dyrr a, at þat var eigi með
minna moti. Enn er hofuð mitt
var comit inn i dyrrin, þa nam
við herðvnum, oc gekk eigi
lengra.'

'I dreamed that I was going into
a house so great and high that
I had never seen one to compare
with it, while the door was in no
lesser proportion. But when my
head was in the doorway the
sides stopped my shoulders, and
I got no further.'

Vol. I, pp. 273–4. At the time that Snorri Sturluson was

arranging to buy Reykjaholt from Magnús Pálsson, one of his household had this dream:

Egil dreymði at Egill Skalla-grimsson kemi at honum, oc var miog vfrynligr. Hann mælti: 'etlar Snorri frendi varr i brott heþan?' 'Þat er mælt', segir Egill. 'Brott ætlar hann, ok þat gerir hann illa,' segir dravm-maðrinn, 'þviat litt hafa menn settið yfir lvt várum Myra-manna, þa er oss timgadiz, oc þurftti hann eigi of-sionvm yfir þessv landi at sia.' Egill qvað visu:

'Seggr sparir sverði at hoggva,
snio-hvitt er bloð lita,
skæru-olld getvm skyra,
scarpr branðr fecc þar landa,
skarpr branðr fecc mer landa.'

Oc sneri þa i brot. En Egill vacnar.

Egill dreamed that Egill Skalla-grimsson came to him, frowning darkly. He said: 'Does our kins-man Snorri intend to move away from here?' 'So it is said', answered Egill. 'He plans to move, and in that he does ill,' said the dream man, 'for men had but little ascendency over the affairs of the men of Mýrar in the days when we were prosperous, and he need not look down with scorn at this homestead.' Egill said a verse:

'The man spares to strike with the sword; blood is white as snow to look at; but I lived through a time of manifest struggle, the sharp sword fur-nished me with land.'

After that he turned away, and Egill awoke.

Vol. 1, p. 285. During the winter after the battle of Viðimýri, a man from Skagafjörðr had this dream:

...hann þottiz koma i hus eitt mikit; þar satv inni conor tvær bloþgar oc rero afram. Honum þotti rigna bloði i liorana. Onnor qvað konan:

'Rom við oc rom við,
rignir bloði,
Gvðr oc Gondvl[1]
fyrir gvma falli.
Við skvllvm raðaz
i Raptahlíð,
þar mvnvm blotadar
oc bolvadar.'

...he dreamed that he came into a big house in which two women were sitting; they were bloody and rocked to and fro. It seemed to him that blood was raining in through the windows. One of the women said:

'We rock and rock. It rains blood in presage of the fall of men; we shall go to Raptahlíð, where we shall be cursed and wounded.'

[1] Valkyr-names.

Vol. 1, p. 432. While riding out against Þórðr and Snorri Þorvaldsson, Sturla Sigvatsson related the following dream to a companion:

...'ek þottumzt hafa mors-bigva hlut i hende, ok var af sniþit sneisar-halldit. Ek þottumzt rétta, ok slita þat i sundr mille handa mer, ok gefa yðr øllum at eta af með mer. Enn vita þottumzt ec, at sea tið var, sem nv er.'

...'I dreamed that I had a piece of sausage in my hand of which the pin-end was cut off. I thought I straightened it, and tore it apart between my hands and gave you all to eat of it with me. I seemed to know that it was at the very same point of time as now.'

Vol. 1, p. 494. At the time of the Melar expedition, Hafliði Höskuldsson had the following dreams:

i

...hann dreymdi at hann var úti staddr á Kolbeinsstöðum; þar átti hann heima í Haugatungu. Hann sá, at leikr var sleginn þar skamt frá garði, ok váru karlar einir at, þat var knattleikr. Þá gekk gráklæddr maðr mikill ofan frá Mý-dal, ok biðu þeir þess at leiknum. Þeir fréttu hann at nafni. Hann kvað:

...he dreamed that he was outside at Kolbeinsstaðir; he had a house there in Haugatunga. He saw that a ball game was going on a little way from the fence, and that men only were there. Then a tall man dressed in grey came down from Mýdalr, and those who were playing waited for him. They asked his name. He said:

'Kár kalla mik,
em ek kominn heðra
heim at skelfa
ok hugi manna,
borgir brjóta
ok boga sveigja,
elda at auka
ok aga at kynda.'

'I am called Kár, I have come here to terrify the world and the minds of men, to demolish castles, to draw bows, to increase animosity and kindle strife.'

'Eða hví leiki þér nú eigi?' Þeir sögðuz øngan hafa knött. 'Hér er', segir hann, ok brá steini undan kuflinum ok laust einn til bana. Síðan tók hverr at öðrum

'But why are you not playing now?' They said that they had no ball. 'Here is one', said he, and whipped a stone from under his cloak and struck a man down.

þann stein ok börðuz með, en allir fellu þeir er fyrir urðu.

Thereupon one after another took this stone and fought with it, and all who were hit fell.

ii

...hann þóttiz vera í Fagraskógi ok þóttiz sjá upp eptir Hítardal, ok sá ríða ofan eptir dalnum flokk manna. Kona fór fyrir liðinu mikil ok illilig ok hafði dúk í hendi ok á rauftrefr niðr ok blæddi ór. Annarr flokkr fór á mót þeim frá Svarfhóli, ok mættuz út frá Hrauni ok börðuz þar. Kona þessi brá dúkinum yfir höfuð þeim, ok er raufin kom á hálsinn, þá kipti hon höfðinu af hverjum þeira. Hon kvað:

...he seemed to be in Fagraskógr, and he thought he looked up along Hítardalr, and saw a company of men riding down through the valley. A tall, grim-looking woman went before them, and had in her hand a cloth from which tatters hung, with blood dripping from them. Another company came toward them from Svarfhóll, and they met out beyond Hraun, and fought there. The woman waved the cloth over their heads, and when the rags touched the neck of each she snatched off his head. She said:

'Veg ek með dreyrgum dúki,
drep ek menn í hyr þenna,
en hlœgir mik œrit
ill vist þar er þeir gista.'

'I kill with a bloody cloth, I drive people into this fight; the poor entertainment where they are staying pleases me.'

Vol. i, p. 515. On the eve of the battle at Ørlygsstaðir, Sturla Þórðarson had this dream:

'Mik dreymdi þat at ek var i Huammi aa fauður-leifð minni, ok þar vero ver allir fyrir hanndan aána upp fra Akri. Kross stoð hia oss aa holltz-mulanum haár ok mikill. Þa þotti mer hlaupa skriða mikil vr fiallinu, ok var smá-griot i allt nema einn steinn; hann var sva mikill, sem hamarr hlypi at oss, ok þótti mer vndir verða margt uaárra manna, ok margt komz vnðan; en Uigfus Iuars son uarð unndir, sva at ek kennda, enn þa uaknaða ek.'

'I dreamed that I was at my ancestral homestead in Hvammr, and that we were all there beyond the river above Akr. A large and tall cross stood near us on a steep mound. Then it seemed to me that a great land-slip ran down the mountain, and it was all in small stones except for one stone; it was as large as if a crag were rushing toward us, and I thought that many of our men were under it, while others of them escaped. I recognized Vígfúss Ívarsson under it, and then I awoke.'

Vol. ii, p. 222. After Hrafn Oddsson and Eyjólfr Þorsteinsson had turned aside to Viðikjörr instead of going on
to attack Gizurr Þorvaldsson, one of Hrafn's men had this
dream:

Þa dreymðe Svarthavfða, at Vig-
fus Gunnsteins son væri horfinn
or liðe þeira, ok reðu sva sumir
menn, at litil mundi verða þessi
ferð vm viga-ferlin. Ok riðu
þeir heim vestr við sva buit.

Then Svarthöfði dreamed that
Vigfúss Gunnsteinsson had disappeared from their band, and
some people interpreted this, that
the expedition would be of little
importance as regards warfare.
At that they rode back to the
west.

Vol. ii, p. 232. While conducting an expedition against Oddr
Þórarinsson, Hrafn Oddsson had the following dream:

Þa dreymde Rafn vm nottina þar
i Forn-haga, at hann þottiz vte
vera, at maðr gecc at honum
mikill. Rafn þottizt spyria, hverr
hann være. Hann qvaz Havstkulldr heita. Rafn spurði: 'hversu
munu fara með oss Odde mala-
ferlin?' Hann svarar: 'sva sem
gliman man fara með ockr'. Þessi
maðr rann a Rafn, ok þottizt hann
i fyrstunne forviða verða, enn
þess at fastare þottiz hann fyrir
verða sem þeir hofðu lengr glimt,
ok Havstkulldr hravcc allt fyrir,
vm þat er lauk.

Hrafn dreamed in the night at
Fornhagi that he was outside, and
that a tall man came to him. Hrafn
thought he asked who he was; he
said he was called Haustskuldr.
Hrafn asked: 'How will it turn
out in the fight between Oddr
and ourselves?' He answered:
'As our wrestling match does'.
This man rushed at Hrafn, and
at first he seemed to himself to
be overmatched, but the longer
they wrestled the firmer he seemed
to grow, and at last Haustskuldr
gave way entirely.

Vol. ii, p. 293. While staying the night in Hvinverjadalr in
the mountains, Þorgils Böðvarsson had this dream:

...honum þótti kona ganga at
húsdurunum mikil, ok hafði barn-
skikkju á herðum; heldr var hon
daprlig. Hon mælti: 'Þar liggr
þú, Þorgils,' segir hon, 'ok muntu
eitt sinn á hurðu liggja síðarr'.
Þorgils vaknaði.

...he dreamed that a tall woman
who had a child's cloak on her
shoulders came to the door of the
house; she was very sad. She
said: 'There you lie, Þorgils, and
you are to lie on a door once
more'. Þorgils awoke.

Sverris Saga. (*Fms.* 8.)

Fms. 8, pp. 7–8. Just before King Sverrir was born, his mother, Gunnhildr, had this dream:

...henni þótti sem hon væri í einu ágætligu lopthúsi, ok þóttist hon léttari verða barns þess er hon gekk með. En þjónustukona hennar sat fyrir knjóm henni, ok skyldi taka við barninu, þegar er fætt væri. Ok er henni þótti sem barnit væri fætt, sló mikilli hræzlu á konu þá er yfir henni sat, ok kallaði á hana ákafliga ok mælti: 'Gunnhildr mín, þú hefir fæddan undarligan burð ok ógurligan sýnum'. III sinnum kallaði hon með hinum sömum orðum. En er hon heyrði konuna kalla svá opt hit sama með skjálfandi röddu, þá forvitnast hon, hvat burði þat væri, er hon hafði fætt; henni sýndist sem þat væri einn steinn vel mikill ok snjóhvítr at lit: en hann glóaði svá mjök, at allavega gneistaði af honum, sem af glóanda járni því, er ákafliga er blásit í afli. En hon mælti svá við þjónustukonu sína: 'gætum við vandliga þessa burðar, ok látum engan mann verða varan við; þvíat flestum man undarligt þikkja er sjá'. Síðan þótti henni sem þær tæki steininn ok legði í einn stól ok hulðu með klæði fögru. En þá er þær höfðu varðveitt þessum steini sem þær vildu, þá flugu þó gneistarnir allavega ígegnum klæðin, ok um allt lopthúsit innan. Þær gerðust mjök hræddar af þessi ógn er þar stóð af: ok síðan vaknaði hon or þeim draumi.

...she thought she was in a fine house and that she was delivered of the child she was carrying. Her serving-woman sat before her and was to receive the child as soon as it was born. And when it seemed to her (Gunnhildr) that the child was born, a great fear seized upon the woman who was with her, and she called aloud to her and said: 'Dear Gunnhildr, you have given birth to an extraordinary infant, awe-inspiring to look upon'. Three times she called out the same words. When Gunnhildr heard the woman saying the same thing so often with trembling voice, she was curious as to what sort of infant she had been delivered of. It seemed to her that it was a rather large stone, snow-white in colour; it shone so that sparks flew in all directions, as with glowing iron, when the hearth is blown up sharply with the bellows. She spoke thus to her serving-woman: 'Let us look after this infant carefully, and let no one know of it, because most people who saw it would think it strange'. After that she thought they took the stone and laid it on a chair and covered it with a fine cloth. When they had attended to the stone as they wished, the sparks flew, nevertheless, in all directions through the cloth, and all about inside the house. They grew very frightened, being filled with awe. After that she woke out of the dream.

Fms. 8, pp. 106–8. Before he attacked Niðaróss (in which onslaught his enemy, Earl Erlingr, was slain, and his forces put to rout), King Sverrir had this dream:

Hann þóttist sofa í einu lopti í bænum, ok vissi hann at nóttin var ljós, ok sá hann mann gánga inn í loptit at þeirri rekkju, er hann hvíldi í, ok mælti: 'rís upp þú, Sverrir, ok gakk með mér!' Honum sýndist þessi maðr ógurligr, ok þóttist ekki öðru treystast, en gera eptir því sem hann bauð. Sá maðr fór upp or bænum, en hann eptir, þar til er þeir komu þar er eldr var fyrir þeim, ok maðr steikðr lá á eldinum. Þá mælti draummaðrinn, at Sverrir skyldi niðr setjast ok matast, ok leggr síðan manninn fyrir hann. (Hann þóttist svara, sem honum var í hug; kvaðst aldri etit hafa rækindi, ok kveðst eigi þá eta myndu. Þá mælti draummaðrinn: 'þú skalt eta, ok þú villt eta, ok svá vill sá er öllu ræðr.') Hann þóttist þá til taka, ok eta holdit af beinunum, ok þótti hverr biti tregt niðr gánga; ok svá lengi sem hann hafði etit, þá þótti honum því minna fyrir, er ofarr var. En er hann kom at höfðinu, vildi hann þá ok eta þat; en sá maðr, er hann leiddi þángat, tók höfuðit til sín; ok kvað hann þá hætta skyldu. Þótti honum þá litlu minna fyrir frá at hverfa, en til at taka fyrir öndverðu, ok varð þá við at skiljast; gengu síðan aptr í bæinn ok til sama innis. Ok er hann þóttist kominn í sömu rekkju, sem hann hafði or risit, þá sá hann leiðtoga sinn gánga út; ok síðan vaknaði hann.

He thought he was sleeping in a loft-room in the town and he knew that the night was light; he saw a man come into the loft and up to the bed in which he was lying. He said: 'Get up, Sverrir, and come with me'. The man seemed grim to him and he dared not do otherwise than as he directed. The man went up out of the town and he followed him until they came to where a fire was before them, with a man roasting in the flames. Then the dream man said that he should sit down and eat. Thereupon he set the man before him. (...) It seemed to him that he then began to eat the flesh of the legs and that each bite went down with an effort, but that the longer he ate the less reluctance he felt, in proportion as he got higher up. When he got to the head he wanted to eat that too, but the man who had taken him there took the head and told him to stop. By that time it seemed to him hardly less difficult to stop than it was to start at the beginning; nevertheless, he had to leave it. After that they went back into the town and to the same room, and when he had got into the same bed which he had left, he saw his guide go out. At that he awoke.

Fms. 8, p. 402. After he had suffered a set-back in a fight against the farmers (*bœndr*) on Rygina mountain, King Sverrir alluded to the following dream:

...hér kom fram draumr, sá er mér birtist, at ek ætta bók, ok var laus öll, ok mikil svá, at hún tók mikit af landínu, ok var stolit or einu kverinu; þar hafa bœndr tekit menn vára.

...now the dream which came to me has been fulfilled: namely, that I thought I had a book which was all unbound, and so large that it took up a great part of the land; a section had been stolen from it; there the farmers captured my (our) men.

þáttr af þorvaldi Víðförla. (*Bks.* 1, pp. 35–50.)

Bks. 1, pp. 39–41. On the three successive nights following the sprinkling of holy water on the stronghold of Koðran Eilífsson's *spámaðr*, Koðran dreamed as follows:

i

...kom spámaðr Koðrans at honum í svefni, ok með daprligri ásjónu ok skjálftafullr, sem af hrezlu, ok mælti til Koðrans: 'illa hefir þú gert, er þú bauðt híngat mönnum þeim, er á svikum sitja við þik, svá at þeir leita at reka mik brottu af bústað mínum, því at þeir steyptu vellanda vatni yfir mitt herbergi, svá at börn mín þola eigi litla kvöl af þeim brennandi dropum, er inna(n) renna um þekjuna; en þó at slíkt skaði sjálfan mik eigi mjök þá er allt at einu þúngt at heyra þyt smábarna, er þau æpa af bruna'.

...Koðran's guardian spirit came to him in a dream, looking sorrowful, and trembling as if with fear, and said: 'You have done ill in that you have invited here men who are plotting to betray you, through trying to drive me from my habitation. They poured boiling water over my house, so that my children suffer no little torture from the burning drops which run down through the roof, and though such does not hurt me much, it is hard, nevertheless, to hear the cries of little children as they scream from the burning'.

ii

...sýndist sá enn flærðarfulli spámaðr Koðrani mjök gagn-staðligr, því sem furr var hann vanr at birtast honum með björtu ok blíðligu yfirliti ok

...the false guardian spirit came before Koðran in a new guise, inasmuch as he was formerly accustomed to appear to him as bright and pleasant-looking and

ágætliga búinn, en nú var hann í svörtum ok herfiligum skinnstakki, dökkr ok illiligr í ásjónu, ok mælti svá til bónda með sorgfullri ok skjálfandi raust: 'Þessir menn stunda fast á at ræna okkr báða okkrum gæðum ok nytsemdum, er þeir vilja elta mik á brottu af minni eiginligri erfð, en svipta þik várri elskuligri umhyggju ok framsýniligum forspám; nú gjör þú svá mannliga, at þú rek þá brottu, svá at vit þarfnimst eigi alla góða luti fyrir þeirra údygð, því at aldri skal ek flýja, en þó er þúngt at þola lengr allar þeirra illgerðir ok úhægindi'.

richly dressed, but now was in a ragged black skin-cloak, and was gloomy and grim-looking; he spoke thus to the man with sorrowful and tremulous voice: 'These men are trying earnestly to rob us both of our treasures and profits, in that they want to drive me away from my proper inheritance, and deprive you of my loving care and foresighted prophecies. Be manful enough to drive them away, so that you and I be not without all good things because of their unworthiness, for I shall never take flight, though it is hard to bear all their evil deeds and unpleasant attentions for long'.

iii

...sá hinn illgjarni andi sýndist bónda um nóttina eptir hit þriðja sinn með hryggiligu yfirbragði, ok bar upp fyrir hann þessháttar kvein með snöktandi röddu, ok segir svá: 'þessi vándr svikari, biskup kristinna manna, hefir afsett mik allri minni eign, herbergi mínu hefir hann spillt, steypt yfir mik vellanda vatni, vætt klæði mín, rifit ok únýtt með öllu, en mér ok mínu hyski hefir hann veitt bótlausan bruna, ok hér með rekit mik nauðgan lángt í brott í auðn ok útlegð. Nú hljótum vit at skilja bæði samvistu ok vinfengi, ok gerist þetta allt af einu saman þínu dygðarleysi. Hugsa þú nú, hverr þitt góz man héðan af varðveita svá dyggiliga, sem ek hefi áðr varðveitt. Þú kallast maðr réttlátr ok trúlyndr, en þú hefir ömbunat mér illu gott'. Þá svarar Koðran: 'ek hefi þik

...the same evil spirit appeared to him the next night, after the third occasion, with a mournful look, and addressed his complaint to him in a whining voice, saying: 'This wicked traitor, the bishop of Christian men, has put me out of all my property, ruined my stronghold, poured boiling water over me, drenched my clothes, torn and spoilt them entirely, and has inflicted irreparable injury by burning upon me and my household, in addition to driving me far away, against my will, into waste places and outlawry. Now we must needs put an end both to our living together and our friendship, and this has all come about through your lack of good faith alone. Think over, now, who will look after your property henceforth as loyally as I have done in the past.

dýrkat svá sem nytsamlígen 'ok styrkan guð, meðan ek var úvitandi ens sanna, en nú, með því at ek hefir reynt þik flærðarfullan ok mjök úmeginn, þá er mér nú rétt ok utan allan glæp at fyrirláta þik, en flýja undir skjól þess guðdóms, er miklu er betri ok styrkari en þú'.—Við þetta skildu þeir, með stygð en engum blíðskap.

You call yourself a man righteous and true, but you have rewarded me evil for good'. Then Koðran answered: 'I worshipped you as a useful and strong god while I was in ignorance concerning the true One, but now, since I have proved you full of deceit and very feeble, it is right for me, and no ill-doing, to turn to the protection of that Godhead who is much stronger and better than you'.—With that they parted in anger, and on no friendly terms.

þáttr Ólafs Geirstaða Álfs. (Fms. 10, pp. 209–15.)

Fms. 10, pp. 210–11. Ólafr Geirstaðaálfr once had the following dream prophetic of a pestilence to come upon his kingdom:

...'mér þótti sem uxi mikill svartr ok illiligr gengi austan á landit; hann fór um allt land mitt ok ríki; mér þótti falla fyrir honum ok hans áblæstri fjöldi manna, svá at mér þótti þat eigi færra en þat sem eptir var; síðast sýndist mér hann drepa hirð mína.'

...'it seemed to me that an ox, large, black and ferocious, came into the country from the east; it went through all my kingdom, and I thought that so many fell before it and its snorting that as many succumbed as were left; it seemed to me that it killed my guard at the last.'

þáttr Orms Storólfssonar. (Fms. 3, pp. 204–28.)

Pp. 222–3. When Ormr Storólfsson was planning how he should avenge the death of his foster-brother, Ásbjörn Virfilsson, he had this dream:

...sá hann, at kona gekk inní tjaldit mikil ok errilig, velbúin ok væn at yfirlitum; hon gekk innar at, þar er Ormr lá, ok nam þar staðar. Ormr þóttist heilsa henni, ok spyrja hana at nafni, en hon kveðst Menglöð heita, dóttir Ófótans norðan or Ófótansfirði, 'en við erum syskin ok Brúsi at föður, en ek átti mennska móður, en móðir hans er sú en kolsvarta

...he saw a fine strong woman, well dressed and beautiful in appearance, come into the tent. She walked in to where Ormr was lying and stopped there. Ormr greeted her, and asked her name; she said she was called Menglöð, daughter of Ófótann from north out of Ófótansfjörðr. 'Brúsi and I are brother and sister on the father's side, but I had a human

ketta, er þar er í hellinum hjá
honum; en þó at við sém skyld,
þá eru við þó ekki lyndis lík;
ræðr hann fyrir eyjunni ytri, ok
er hon sýnu betri; veitir hann
mér þúngar búsifjar, svá at ek
hygg, at ek muna í brottu stökkva;
veit ek ok hvert eyrindi þitt er,
þú ætlar at hefna Ásbjarnar fóst-
bróður þíns, ok er þat vorkunn,
þvíat þú átt eptir hraustan mann
at mæla; mun þér ok forvitni á
at vita, hversu honum var í hel
komit, en þar munu ekki margir
kunna frá at segja, utan Brúsi ok
ek'. Hóf hon þá upp alla sögu,
ok sagði frá lífláti Ásbjarnar, ok
svá kvað hon allar þær vísur, er
hann hafði kveðit, 'en eigi þik-
jumst ek þar sjá fyrir mun um,
hvort meira má tröllskapr Brúsa
ok móður hans eðr hamíngja þín,
en öngvan mann óttast hann utan
þik einn, ok viðrbúnat hefir hann
veittan, ef þú kynnir at koma;
hann hefir fært þat bjarg í hellis-
dyrnar, at ekki má í hellinn
komast, meðan þat stendr þar, en
þó at þú sér sterkr, þá hefir þú
hvorki afl við Brúsa, né bjarginu
í brott at koma; nú eru hér glófar
at ek vil gefa þér, ok fylgir sú
náttúra, at þeim verðr aldri afla-
fátt, sem þá hefir á höndum; yrði
þat svá at þú ynnir Brúsa, þá
vilda ek at þú gæfir Sauðey í vald
mér, en ek mun heldr vera þér
í sinni, þvíat mér er þú vel í
þokka, þóat við megim eigi
njótast sakir trúar þinnar'. Síðan
hvarf konan en Ormr vaknaði,
ok voru þar glófarnir, en hann
mundi allar vísurnar.

mother while his mother is that
coal-black cat who lives in the
cave with him. Though we are
related we are not alike in disposition; he rules over the outer
island, which is much the better;
he is a bad neighbour to me so
that I am thinking of running
away; and I know what your
errand is: you intend to avenge
Ásbjörn, your foster-brother, and
that is excusable, since you right
the case of a valiant man; you will
be interested to know how he was
killed, but not many will be able
to tell, except Brúsi and I.' Then
she told the whole story, and
described Ásbjörn's death, and
repeated all the verses which he
had recited. 'I cannot foresee
whether the wizardry of Brúsi
and his mother or your guardian
spirit will be the more powerful,
but he fears no man except you
alone, and he has made prepara-
tion in case you should come; he
has placed such a boulder in the
cave-door that no one can get in
while it stands there; though you
are strong you have not enough
strength to match yourself against
Brúsi, nor to move the boulder.
Now here are gloves which I will
give you; they have the characteristic that he who has them on
never lacks strength. If it be so
that you defeat Brúsi, then I
should like you to give Sauðey
into my power; I shall help you
for you are very pleasing to me,
though we may not enjoy each
other on account of your faith.'
After that the woman vanished,
but Ormr awoke and the gloves
were there; he remembered all
the verses.

þórleifs þáttr Jarlsskálds. (*Fj. Ísl. þættir*, pp. 383–99.)

Fj. Ísl. þættir, pp. 397–8. Hallbjörn of Þingvellir once attempted to compose a poem about a dead poet on his burial mound, with the following result:

Síðan sofnar hann; ok eftir þat sér hann, at opnast haugrinn, ok gengr þar út maðr, mikill vexti, ok vel búinn. Hann gekk upp á hauginn at Hallbirni, ok mælti: 'Þar liggr þú Hallbjörn, ok vildir þú fást í því, sem þér er ekki lánat, at yrkja lof um mik; ok er þat annathvárt, at þér verðr lagit í þessi íþrótt, ok muntú þat af mér fá, meira enn vel flestum mönnum öðrum, ok er þat vænna, (at) svá verði, ella þarftú ekki í þessu at brjótast lengr. Skal ek nú kveða fyrir þér vísu, ok ef þú getr numit vísuna, ok kant hana, þá er þú vaknar, þá munt þú verða þjóðskáld, ok yrkja lof um marga höfðingja; ok mun þér í þessi íþrótt mikit lagit verða'. Síðan togar hann á honum tunguna, ok kvað vísu þessa:

'Hér liggr skáld þats skálda
skörungr vas mestr at flestu;
naddveiti frák nýtan
níð Hákoni smíða.
áðr gat engr né síðan
annarra svá manna,
frægt hefir orðit þat firðum,
férám lokit hánum.'

'Nú skaltú svá hefja skáldskapinn, at þú skalt yrkja lofkvæði um mik, þá er þú vaknar, ok vanda sem mest, bæði hátt ok orðfœri ok einna mest kenningar.' Síðan hverfr hann aftr í hauginn, ok lykst hann aftr; enn Hallbjörn vaknar.

Then he fell asleep; after that he saw that the howe opened and a tall and well-dressed man came out. He went up on to the howe to Hallbjörn and said: 'There you lie, Hallbjörn, working over something you are not fitted for—the composing of a poem in praise of me. It shall be one way or the other, either, as is likely, you shall be given skill above most others, which you shall get from me, or you need not struggle any more with it. Now I shall recite a verse to you, and if you learn it, and remember it when you wake, you will become a great skald, and compose poems in praise of many chiefs; you will be very highly accomplished in this art'. Next he pulled his tongue and said this verse:

'Here lies the skald who in most respects was the greatest in power among skalds. I have heard that the distinguished man composed a libel on Hákon; no one else thus requited him his plunder of goods either before or since; this has been much talked of among men.'

'You shall begin your poetic career by composing a poem in praise of me when you awake; take the greatest care with the metre and style, and most of all with the kennings.' At that he turned back into the howe and shut it. But Hallbjörn awoke.

Þorskfirðinga Saga.

Pp. 8–9. On his way to Agnarr's howe, Þórir Oddsson had this dream:

...maðr kom at honum, mikill, í rauðum kyrtli ok hafði hjálm á höfði ok sverð búit í hendi; hann hafði um sik digrt belti ok þar á góðan kníf ok glófa á höndum; var þessi maðr mikilúðlegr og virðulegr. Hann mælti reiðulega til Þóris ok stakk á honum döggskónum ok bað hann vaka ok mælti: 'Ills manns efni ertu, er þú vill ræna frændr þína; enn ek vil', sagði hinn komni maðr, 'gera til þín verðleikum betr, því at ek em bróðir feðr þíns ok sammæðr við hann; ek vil gefa þér gjafir til þess, at þú hverfir aftr ok leitir annarra féfanga. Þú skalt þiggja at mér kyrtil góðan þann er þér man hlífa við eldi ok vápnum, ok þar með hjálm ok sverð. Ek skal ok gefa þér glófa þá, er þú mant enga fá slíka, því at liði þínu mun óklaksárt verða, ef þú strýkr þeim með; þessa glófa skaltu á höndum hafa, þá er þú bindr sár manna, ok man skjótt verk ór taka. Kníf ok belti læt ek hér eftir, ok þat skaltu jafnan á þér hafa. Ek mun ok gefa þér tuttugu merkr gulls ok tuttugu merkr silfrs'. Þórir þóttist svara, at honum þótti þetta of lítit af svá nánum frænda ok færíkum, ok lézt eigi aftr munu hverfa við litla fémútu, 'vissa ek eigi', segir Þórir, 'at troll væri mér svá nær í ætt, áðr þú sagðir mér. Enn engrar eirðar ættir þú af mér ván, ef eigi væri frændsemi með okkr'. Agnarr segir: 'Seint munu þín

...a big man dressed in a red tunic and having a helmet on his head, and an ornamented sword in his hand, came to him; he had about him a thick belt in which there was a good knife, and gloves on his hands; the man was imposing and stately. He spoke angrily to Þórir, thrust at him with the tip of the chape, told him to wake up, and said: 'You are a poor sort of man, if you want to rob your kinsman; but', said the newcomer, 'I shall treat you better than you deserve, because I am a half-brother of your father, and am born of the same mother. I will give you gifts on condition that you turn back and seek booty elsewhere. You shall have from me this good tunic which will protect you against fire and weapons, and with it a helmet and sword. I shall also give you these gloves whose like you will never find, for your followers will be hard to injure if you stroke them with them; you shall have these gloves on your hands when you bind up the wounds of men and the pain will be taken away quickly. I shall leave the knife and belt behind and you must always wear them. I shall also give you twenty marks of gold, and twenty marks of silver'. It seemed to Þórir that he answered that he thought this too little from so near and rich a kinsman, and declared he would not turn back for a small

augu fyld verða á fénu, ok því máttu vorkynna mér', sagði Agnarr, 'at mér þykki féit gott, því at þú munt ærit mjök elska féit áðr lýkr'. Þórir segir: 'Ekki hirði ek um illspár þínar; enn þiggja vil ek, at þú vísir mér til meiri févánar, ef þú vilt þitt fé undan þiggja'. 'Heldr vil ek þat', segir Agnarr, 'enn deila illdeildum við þik. Valr hét víkingr, er átti gull mikit; hann bar féit undir helli einn norðr við Dumbshaf ok lagðist á síðan ok synir hans með honum, ok urðu allir at flugdrekum; þeir hafa hjálma á höfðum ok sverð undir bægslum. Nú er hér kalkr, er þú skalt drekka af tvá drykki, enn förunautr þinn einn, enn þá verðr eftir þat er má.' Síðan vaknar Þórir, ok váru þessir hlutir allir þar í hjá honum, er Agnarr gaf honum.

bribe. 'I did not know', said Þórir, 'that a troll was so closely related to me before you told me; but you would have had no mercy to expect from me if it had not been for our relationship.' Agnarr replied: 'But late will your eyes have their fill of treasure, and you may understand that my property seems good to me, because you will yourself love precious things enough before the end'. Þórir said: 'I do not care about your evil prophecies, but I will accept that you point out to me where I may have greater expectation of treasure if you want to have yours spared'. 'I would rather do that', said Agnarr, 'than quarrel with you. A viking was named Valr who had much gold. He put it into a cave north by the Polar Sea (Dumbshaf) and settled himself upon it, and all his sons with him, and they all became flying dragons; they have helmets on their heads and swords sheathed under their wings. Here is a cup from which you shall drink two draughts, and your companion one, but you must leave whatever may be over.' Afterwards Þórir awoke, and found all the things that Agnarr gave him by his side.

P. 9. Þórir then took two draughts from the cup and his companion one. There was still some left, so Þórir drained the cup and then fell asleep:

Agnarr kom þá enn ok ávítaði Þóri, er hann hafði alt af drukkit kalkinum, ok kvað hann þess drykkjar gjalda mundu hinn síðara hlut æfi sinnar. Agnarr segir þeim fyrir marga hluti þá

At that Agnarr came again and rebuked Þórir for having drunk all there was in the cup, and said he would suffer for this drink in the latter part of his life. Agnarr told him of many things which

er fram kómu síðar, ok lagði ráð til með Þóri, hversu hann skyldi vinna hellinn Vals víkings.

were to come to pass in the future, and planned with Þórir how he was to break open the cave of the viking, Valr.

Þorsteins Saga Síðu-Hallssonar.

Pp. 13–16. Þórhaddr Hafljótsson once had twelve dreams, and amongst them these four:

i

'Sá var draumr minn enn fimti, at ek þóttumst ganga til sjávar, þar sem var saltsviða mikil, ok synir mínir með mér ok þóttumst ek eta glóandi salt ok drekka sjáinn við.'

'It was my fifth dream that I thought I was going to the sea to a place where there was a great salt-burning, and my sons with me. It seemed to me that I ate red-hot salt and drank the sea with it.'

ii

'Sá var draumr minn enn átti, at mér þótti tungan svo löng í mér, at ek þóttumst krækja henni aftr á hnakkann ok fram í munninn öðrum megin.'

'It was my eighth dream that I thought my tongue was so long that I wound it round the back of my neck, and forward into my mouth on the other side.'

iii

'Sá er hinn níundi draumr minn, at ek þóttumst vera á fjalli því er Gerpir heitir. Þat fjall er í Austfjörðum, ok þaðan sá ek um mörg lönd, enn hvergi í nánd mér, því at myrkri laust yfir alt.'

'It was my ninth dream that I thought I was on the mountain which is called Gerpir. This mountain is in the district of the Eastfirths, and from there I saw over many lands, but nothing at all near me, because darkness suddenly closed down over everything.'

iv

'Sá var enn tólfti draumr minn, at ek þóttumst fara ór Breiðdal Hjarðarskarð, ok til bæjar þess er í Þroti heitir, ok þótti mér sem ekkja nökkur byggi þar ok þóttumst ek drepa fótum í þúfu ok falla, enn mér þótti Þorsteinn ríða um þvera götuna í móti mér.'

'It was my twelfth dream that I thought I went from Breiðdalr over Hjarðarskarð to a homestead which is called Þrot, and it seemed to me that a certain widow lived there: I thought I stumbled against a hummock and fell, and that Þorsteinn was riding across the track toward me.'

P. 20. Before Þorsteinn finally decided to take vengeance upon Þórhaddr, he had the following dream:

...dreymdi at Jóreiðr móðir hans kom at honum; hon var Þiðranda-dóttir, enn hon var þá önduð. Hon spurði: 'Ætlar þú nú brátt til sættarfundar við Þórhadd?' Hann kvaðst eigi þat hafa í hug sér. 'Viltu hefna þá?' sagði hon. Hann kvaðst þat hugsat hafa. Hon mælti: 'Eigi þarftu þá lengr at fresta, þvi at eigi mun fyrri niðr falla illmælit enn hefndin fer fram', ok kvað þá vera ráð um daginn eftir—'tak ok öxar þínar báðar, Jarlsnaut ok Þiðrandanaut, ok haf þá í hendi til hefndanna, er þyngri er í hendi, því at Þiðranda-nautr hefir oft vel gefizt, þótt hon sé eigi jafn-fögr sem hin'. Síðan vaknar hann.

...he dreamed that Jóreiðr, his mother, came to him; she was the daughter of Þiðrandi, and was then dead. She asked: 'Do you intend to have a meeting of reconciliation with Þórhaddr soon?' Þorsteinn said that he did not have that in mind. 'Will you avenge yourself?' said she. He answered that he had thought of that. She replied: 'Then you need not put it off any longer, because the slander will not be hushed until the revenge is accomplished', and said this would be a wise plan for the next day—'take both your axes, Jarlsnaut (Earl's gift) and Þiðrandanautr (Þiðrandi's gift), and carry in your hand the one which is the heavier, for Þiðrandanautr has often been of good service, though it be not as beautiful as the other'. After that he awoke.

Pp. 24–6. Before he was murdered by his Irish thrall, Þorsteinn Síðuhallsson had the following dreams on three successive nights:

i

Konur þrjár kvámu at honum ok mæltu við hann: 'Vaki þú, Þor-steinn,' sögðu þær, 'Gilli þræll þinn vill svíkja þik fyrir þat er þú lézt gelda hann, ok er þetta eigi lygi; láttu drepa hann', sögðu þær. Þá kvað ein þeira, sú er fyrst gekk, vísu þessa ok var harmþrungin:

'Allskörpu hefr orpit
ævin-Hildr með lævi

Three women came to him and spoke: 'Wake up, Þorsteinn,' said they, 'Gilli, your thrall, will deal treacherously with you because you had him castrated, and this is no lie; kill him'. Then the one among them who walked before the others said this verse, and was sorrowful:

'Life's goddess of battle has treacherously thrown a very

fyr herðöndum hurðar
heinar ægis beini;
gumnum stendr fyr gamni
Gerðr með brugðnu sverði,
villat enn með öllu
ey, kvæn, Heðins þeyjar
ey, kvæn, Heðins þeyjar.'
...þá vaknaði Þorsteinn ok lét
leita þrælsins ok fanst hann eigi.

hard stone on the warrior's
path; the goddess of battle
continually stands in the way
of men's joy with her drawn
sword; she is still utterly un-
willing to do anything better.'

...Then Þorsteinn woke and
searched for the thrall, and he was
not found.

ii

...kvámu draumkonurnar með
hina sömu sögu, ok gekk sú fyrst,
er áðr var í miðju, ok kvað sú
þetta, er fyrst gekk:

'Framm gekk, dóms, at dómi
dómspakr, hinns lög rakði,
unni guð þess er inni
óþekð skyli slekkja,
áðr fleinþinga fengi
fangsæl Dvalins hanga
Baldr, sás blóðs of eldi,
biðkvæn und lok, riðnar
biðkvæn und lok, riðnar.'
(.   .   .   .   .)
Þorsteinn vaknaði ok var leitat
þrælsins ok fanst hann eigi.

...the dream women came to
him with the same story, and that
one walked first who had before
been in the middle; the one who
came first said this verse:

'Forward to doom went the
skilful judge who understood
the law; God grant the administrator of justice that he be
able to quench the ill-will
against him, before Hel, rich
in spoil, can prevail against the
warrior, he who swings (?) the
sword.'
(.   .   .   .   .)
Þorsteinn woke and the thrall was
hunted for and was not found.

iii

...þær kvámu enn ok váru þá
grátandi allar; gekk sú þá fyrst,
er áðr hafði síðast gengit. Sú
mælti þá: 'Hvert skulum vér þá
hverfa eftir þinn dag, Þorsteinn?'
sagði hon. Hann svarar: 'Til
Magnúss sonar míns', sagði hann.
'Litla stund munu vér þar mega
vera', sagði hon ok kvað þá vísu:

'Flugvörum sitr fjörnis
fá kund meginunda

...the women came again and
were then all weeping. That one
was first who had before been
last. She said: 'Where shall we
turn after your day, Þorsteinn?'
He answered: 'To my son Magnús'. 'We shall be allowed to
stay with him but a short time',
said she, and spoke this verse:

'The bright axe, sharp for
head-wounds, rests over the

hvöss of höggnum vísa
hjálma gríðr at jálmi,
þess er endr fyr enda
andþings of sjöt banda
(þat mun ógurligt) ægis
ós skýmáni tóku
ós skýmáni tóku.'

chieftain's hewn son, who
never fled in battle—it will
be dreadful—he, whom the
meeting with the frightful one
formerly put to death; the
waning moon waxed in the
heavens.'

(. . . . .)
Eftir þetta lét Þorsteinn ok
Yngvildr kona hans leita Gilla,
enn hann hittist eigi.

(. . . . .)
After this Þorsteinn and Yngvildr,
his wife, searched for Gilli, but
he was not met with.

Þorsteins Saga Víkingssonar. (*Fas.* II, pp. 55–112.)

Fas. II, p. 77. Þorsteinn Víkingsson once had the following
dream:

'Mik dreymdi, at hingat runnu
þrjá tigi vargar, ok vóru sjau
bjarndýr ok hinn áttundi rauð-
kinni; hann var mikill ok grimmlegr, ok at auk tvær refkeilur;
þær fóru fyrir flokkinum, ok
vóru heldr illilegar, ok á þeim
var mér mestr óþokki. Vargarnir
sóttu at oss allir, ok þótti mér
þar koma um síðir, at þeir rifu
í sundr alla brœðr mína nema þik
einn, ok þó felltu. Marga þótti
mér vér drepa björnuna, enn alla
drap ek vargana ok hina minni
refkeiluna, enda fell ek þá.'

'I dreamed that thirty wolves ran
hither; with them were seven bears
and an eighth with red chaps; he
was large and fierce. In addition,
there were two vixens who led
the pack and were very vicious-
looking; these seemed the most
unpleasant to me. All the wolves
attacked us, and at last it came to
this, that they tore to pieces all my
brothers except you, but, nevertheless, you fell. I thought that
we killed many of the bears and
that I killed all the wolves and the
smaller vixen; then I fell.'

Þórsteins þáttr Uxafóts. (*Fj. Ísl. þættir,* pp. 438–66.)

Fj. Ísl. þættir, pp. 448–51. Þórsteinn Uxafótr once slept on a
burial mound and dreamed as follows:

'Mér þótti haugr sjá opnast, ok
gekk þar út ór maðr rauðklæddr;
hann var mikill maðr vexti, ok
ekki aðalliga illiligr.' Hann gekk
at Þórsteini ok heilsaði upp á
hann. Þórsteinn tók honum vel
ok spurði hann at nafni eðr hvar

'It seemed to me that the howe
opened and a man dressed in red
came out; he was large of build
and not wholly forbidding. He
went to Þórsteinn and greeted
him. Þórsteinn received him
pleasantly and asked his name

hann ætti heima. Hann lézt Brynjarr heita ok eiga heima í haugi þeim, "er þú sér standa hér í dalnum. Enn veit ek, hvat þú heitir ok svá hvers kyns þú ert, ok svá þat, at þú mant mikill maðr verða fyrir þér, eðr viltú fara með mér ok sjá hýbýli mín?" Þórsteinn játaði því ok stóð upp ok tók öxi sína, er Þórkell hafði gefit honum; ganga inn í hauginn. Enn er Þórsteinn kom þar, sýndist honum þar vel fyrirbúit. Hann sá þar til hœgri handar sitja ellifu menn á bekk. Þeir váru allir rauðklæddir ok heldr fáligir. Öðrumegin í hauginum sá hann sitja tólf menn. Þeir váru allir bláklæddir. Sá var (einn) þeira mestr ok illiligr. Brynjarr laut at Þórsteini ok mælti: "Sá er bróðir minn, hinn mikli maðr, ok erum vit þó ekki skaplíkir; hann heitir Oddr ok vill flestum illt; hann veitir mér þungar búsifjár; enn hann er því öllu sterkari enn ek, sem hann er meiri vöxtum; enn ek hefi orðit at játta því ok mínir menn, at fá honum hverja nátt mörk gulls eðr tvær merkr silfrs, eðr einhvern grip jafnan þessu. Hefir nú svá fram farit hinn næsta mánuð ok gerumst vér nú farnir at lausafé. Oddr hefir at varðveita gull þat, er sú náttúra fylgir, at hverr maðr, sem mállaus er ok leggr þat undir tungurœtr sér, þá tekr þegar mál sitt, ok af því gulli má móðir þín mál fá; enn Oddr geymir þat svá ríkt, at þat gengr aldri af honum hvárki nótt né dag". Nú sezt Brynjarr niðr hjá sínum kumpánum, enn Þórsteinn sitr þeira yztr. Enn er þeir hafa setit um hríð, stóð Brynjarr upp ok gekk yfir at Oddi bróður

and where he lived. He said he was called Brynjarr and lived in the howe "which you see standing here in the valley. But I know what your name is and of what family you are, and also that you will be a great man; will you come with me and see my house?" Þórsteinn agreed to this and stood up and took the axe which Þórkell had given him. They went into the howe, and when Þórsteinn came in, it seemed to him that it was well furnished. He saw eleven men sitting on a bench on the right hand. They were all dressed in red, and rather quiet. He saw twelve men sitting on the other side of the howe. They were all dressed in blue, and one among them was taller and more forbidding than the rest. Brynjarr leant toward Þórsteinn and said: "The tall man is my brother, but we are, nevertheless, not alike in temper. He is named Oddr, and wishes ill to most people. He is a bad companion to me; but he is as much stronger than I as he is larger in build; I, and my men as well, have been forced to get him one mark of gold or two marks of silver, or some treasure of equal value, every night. This has gone on for the last month and we are almost at the end of our resources. Oddr has in his keeping a gold ring which is of such a nature that every mute person immediately gets power of speech when he lays it under the root of his tongue, and from this ring your mother may get her power of speech; but Oddr guards it so carefully that it is off him neither

sínum, ok afhendi honum einn
hring digran. Oddr tók við þeg-
jandi, enn Brynjarr gekk aftr til
sætis síns. Svá stóð upp hverr at
öðrum, ok fœrðu Oddi allir nökkurn grip, enn hann gaf engum
þökk í móti. Enn er þeir höfðu
þetta allir (gert), þá mælti Brynjarr: "Þat mun þér ráð, Þórsteinn,
at gera sem aðrir ok fœra Oddi
nökkurt gjald; eigi mun annat
duga með því at þú sitr a várn
bekk". Oddr var ýgldr mjök, ok
sat upp mjök gneypr ok heldr
ófrýniligr. Þórsteinn stóð þá upp
ok helt á öxi sinni. Hann gekk
yfir at Oddi ok mælti: "Ekki
er ek plaggamargr til, Oddr, at
lúka þér gjald þetta; muntú ok
ekki mikilþægr at við mik, því
at ek er óríkr". Oddr anzaði ok
heldr stutt: "Ekki er mér um
kvámu þína hingat, enn muntú
eigi frammi láta þat er þér líkar?"
"Ek hefi ekki til nema öxi mína, ef
þú vilt hana taka", (segir Þórsteinn). Oddr rétti höndina í
móti, enn Þórsteinn höggr til
hans; kemr þat í höndina ofan
ölnboga ok tekr af. Oddr sprettr
þá upp ok allir þeir, er (í)
hauginum váru; vápn þeira hengu
uppi yfir þeim; grípa þeir þau;
slœr nú með þeim í bardaga.
Þat sér Þórsteinn, at nú er ekki
fjarri um með þeim, Þórsteini ok
Oddi, er Oddr var einhendr.
Allir lítast honum hinir bláklæddu
menn harðfengari; þat sér hann
ok, þó at þeir höggist af hendr eðr
fœtr eðr særist öðrum stórsárum,
þá eru þeir á annarri stundu heilir.
Enn þat er Þórsteinn hjó, þá var
þat eftir eðli. Eigi linti Þórsteinn
fyrr, ok þeir Brynjarr allir saman,
enn Oddr var drepinn ok þeir

night nor day". Then Brynjarr
sat down by his companions, and
Þórsteinn sat outermost of them.
When they had sat for a while,
Brynjarr got up and went over
to Oddr, his brother, and handed
him a thick ring. Oddr took it in
silence, and Brynjarr went back
to his place; in the same way his
companions got up, one after the
other, and brought Oddr some
treasure, but he thanked none of
them. When they all had done
this, Brynjarr said: "It is best,
Þórsteinn, for you to do as the
others, and offer some tribute to
Oddr; nothing else will do, as you
are sitting on our bench". Oddr
was very angry, and was much
bent forward and fiercely frowning. Þórsteinn then stood up
and held fast to his axe. He went
over to Oddr, and said: "I have
not enough with me, Oddr, to
yield this tribute up to you; also,
you must not be exacting with
me, for I am poor". Oddr
answered, and very shortly: "I
do not like your coming here,
but will you not bring forward
what you think suitable?" "I
have nothing except my axe, if
you will take that", said Þórsteinn. Oddr stretched out his
arm to take it, and Þórsteinn
struck at him; the blow caught
the arm above the elbow and
took it off. Oddr and all those
who were in the howe sprang up;
their weapons were hanging up
above them; they seized them
and battle broke out. Þórsteinn
saw that there was not such an
uneven match between himself
and Oddr, since he had only one
arm; all the men dressed in blue

allir kumpánar. Þórsteinn var þá
mjök móðr, enn ekki sárr, því at
Brynjarr ok hans félagar höfðu
hlíft Þórsteini við höggum öllum.
Brynjarr tók nú gullit af Oddi
dauðum ok fekk Þórsteini, ok
bað hann fœra móður sinni. Hann
gaf honum tólf merkr silfrs í
sjóði ok mælti: "Mikit frelsi hefir
þú unnit mér, Þórsteinn, því at
nú ræð ek hér haugi ok eignum;
mun þetta upphaf þinna þrek-
virkja, er þú munt vinna útan-
lendis. Þú munt ok taka siða-
skifti, ok er sá siðr miklu betri,
þeir sem hann mega hljóta, enn
hinum er erfiðara um, sem eigi
eru til þess skapaðir ok slíkir eru
sem ek, því at vit brœðr várum
jarðbúar. Nú þœtti mér miklu
máli skifta, at þú kœmir nafni
mínu undir skírn, ef þér yrði þat
auðit at eiga son". Síðan leiddi
hann mik út ór hauginum, ok
áðr vit skildum mælti hann:
"Ef mín orð mega nökkut, þá
snúist þér þín verk öll til heiðrs ok
hamingju". Eftir þat snøri Bryn-
jarrinn í hauginn, enn ek vaknaða;
ok þat til marks um, at hér er nú
bæði hjá mér sjóðrinn ok gullit.'

seemed to him to be the more
valiant; he saw, too, that, though
they cut each others' hands and
feet off or gave each other serious
wounds, they were whole again
the next moment; but when
Þórsteinn struck, the natural consequences followed. Þórsteinn,
together with Brynjarr and his
followers, did not stop before
Oddr and all his band were killed.
By that time Þórsteinn was very
tired; but he was not wounded
because Brynjarr and his com-
rades had shielded him against all
the blows. Brynjarr now took
Oddr's gold ring, as he lay dead,
gave it to Þórsteinn, and told him
to bring it to his mother (Þórsteinn's). He gave him twelve
marks of silver in a purse, and
said: "You have won me great
freedom, Þórsteinn, for now I
alone am in authority over the
howe and property; this will be
the first of your deeds of prowess
in foreign lands. You shall also
submit to a change of faith, and
it will be better for those who
receive it than for those who
resist it, who are not destined
for this, and are as I am, for
we brothers were earth-dwellers;
now, it would seem to me of great
importance that you should bring
my name under baptism, if it be
fated for you to have a son!"
After that he led me out of the
howe, and before we parted he
said: "If my words mean anything, all your activities will turn
to honour and good fortune".
Then Brynjarr turned back into
the howe and I awoke, and, as a
token, here are both the purse
and the gold beside me.'

Þórðar Saga Hræðu.

P. 19. Before a fray in a booth over a cloak he had purchased,
Þórðr Hræða had this dream:

'Þat dreymdi mik, at ek þottumst
kominn til Hvítár í Borgarfirði
ok eiga tal við útlenda menn, eigi
sízt um kaup nökkur; ok í því
kómu í búðina vargar margir, ok
var mér mikill viðbjóðr við þeim;
síðan réðu þeir á mik ok vildu
drepa mik ok rifu af mér klæðin,
enn ek brá sverðinu ok hjó ek í
sundr einn varginn í miðju ok
höfuðit af öðrum; síðan hlupu at
mér vargarnir öllum megin, enn
ek þóttumst verjast, ok varð ek
mjök móðr, ok eigi þóttumst ek
vita, hversu mér myndi vegna.
Í því hljóp fram fyrir mik einn
bjarnhúnn ok vildi verja mik, ok
í því vaknaða ek.'

'I dreamed that I had come to
White River in Burgfirth and
that I talked with foreign men,
especially about some bargain;
at that moment many wolves
came into the booth, and they
filled me with disgust; then they
attacked me, and wanted to kill
me, and tore off my clothes; but
I drew my sword and cut one of
the wolves asunder through the
middle, and hewed the head off
another. Next, the wolves rushed
upon me from all sides, but I
thought I defended myself; I became very exhausted and did not
know how it would turn out
for me. At that time a bear's cub
leaped before me, and wanted to
defend me, and with that I
awoke.'

Vápnfirðinga Saga.

Pp. 25–6. Before Brodd-Helgi and his son were slain in an
ambush, Brodd-Helgi's foster-mother had this dream:

'Þat dreymdi mik, at mér þótti
hér upp rísa at Hofi uxi einn
bleikr at lit, mikill ok skrautlegr,
ok bar hann hátt hornin, ok gekk
á sandinn fram hjá Sunnudals-
mynni. Enn sá ek fara naut utar
eftir heraðinu, stór ok eigi allfá,
ok þar fyrir uxi rauðflekkóttr,
eigi mikill né fagr, enn allster-
klegr var hann. Nautin stönguðu
uxann til bana, hinn mikla. Þá
reis hér upp at Hofi rauðr uxi,
ok var beinalitr á hornum; hann
var allra nauta skrautlegastr. Sá

'I dreamed that a fawn-coloured
ox, large and magnificent, appeared here at Hof; he carried
his horns high, and went forward
on the shore near Sunnudalr's
end. Then I saw cattle, large,
and in no small number, going
further out along the country-
side, and before them a red-roan
ox, neither big nor handsome,
but very strong. The cattle gored
the great ox to death. Then a red
ox, with horns the colour of
ebony, appeared, which was the

stangaði rauðflekkótta uxann til bana. Þá reis upp í Krossavík þjór nökkur, ok var sænautalitr á honum. Hann fór beljandi um alt heraðit ok heiðarnar ok leitaði ávalt hins rauða uxans: enda vaknaða ek þá.'

most magnificent of all cattle. He gored the red-roan ox to death. Then a bull came to light, in Krossavík, which was the colour of a sea-cow. He went bellowing about all the district and the heaths, searching constantly for the red ox; then I awoke.'

Vatnsdæla Saga.

P. 90. Þorsteinn Ingimundarson was once warned in a dream not to attend a certain feast:

...ena þriðju nótt áðr Þorsteinn skyldi heiman ríða, dreymdi hann, at kona sú, er fylgt hafði þeim frændum, kom at honum, ok bað hann hvergi fara; hann kvaðst heitit hafa. Hon mælti: 'Þat lízt mér óvitrlegra, ok þú munt ok illt af hljóta,'—ok svá fór þrjár nætr at hon kom, ok ávítaði hann, ok kvað honum eigi hlýða mundu, ok tók á augum hans.

...the third night before Þorsteinn was to ride from home, he dreamed that the woman who was the guardian spirit of the family came to him and told him not to go; he said he had promised. She answered: 'It seems to me very unwise, and evil will result to you from it'; she came to him thus for three nights, and warned him, and said he should not accept the invitation, and touched his eyes.

Víga-Glúms Saga.

Pp. 25–6. At the time of his grandfather's death, Víga-Glúmr had the following dream:

Hann þóttist vera úti staddr á bæ sínum ok sjá út til fjarðarins. Hann þóttist sjá konu eina ganga utan eftir heraðinu ok stefndi þangat til Þverár; enn hon var svá mikil, at axlirnar tóku út fjöllin tveggja vegna. Enn hann þóttist ganga ór garði á mót henni, ok bauð henni til sín. Ok síðan vaknaði hann.

He thought he was outside at his homestead, looking towards the firth, and that he saw a woman stalking out along the countryside, and coming in the direction of Þverá. She was so big that her shoulders overtopped the mountains on both sides. It seemed to him that he went out of the homestead to meet her and invited her to his house. After that he awoke.

Pp. 59–60. While living in anticipation of an attack, Víga-Glúmr had these two dreams:

i

'Ek hugðumst ganga hér ór garði einnsaman ok slyppr, enn mér þótti Þórarinn ganga at móti mér, ok hafa harðstein mikinn í hendi; ok þóttumst ek vanbúinn við fundi okkrum. Ok er ek hugðak at, sá ek annan harðstein hjá mér, ok réðumst ek í mót. Ok er við fundumst, þá vildi hvárr ljósta annan; enn steinarnir kómu saman, ok varð af brestr hár.' Már spyrr: 'Hvárt þótti þér heita mega híbýlabrestr?' Glúmr svarar: 'Meiri var enn svá'. 'Þótti þér heita mega heraðsbrestr?' Glúmr svarar: 'Vel er því til jafnat, því at ek þóttumst vita, at heyrði um alt heraðit. Ok er ek vaknaða, kvað ek vísu:

"Harðsteini lét húna
harðgeðr Limafjarðar
—þat sák dóms í draumi—
dyn-Njarðr mik of barðan,
enn ek þrádáttar þóttumk
þjósti keyrðr of ljósta
sævar-hrafns í svefni
snarr beinanda steini".'

'I thought I was going out of the homestead here, alone and unarmed, and that Þórarinn was coming toward me, and had a large whetstone in his hand; I felt unprepared for our meeting. As I was thinking this, I saw another whetstone near me, and I turned to it (for a weapon). When we met, each one wanted to strike the other, but the stones came together with a loud crash.' Már asked: 'Did you think it might be called a crash heard all over the homestead?' Glúmr answered: 'It was louder than that'. 'Did you think it might be called a crash heard all over the district?' Glúmr replied: 'That is a good comparison, for it seemed to me certain that it was heard over all the country-side; and when I awoke I said a verse:

"The hard-hearted warrior struck me with a whetstone— I saw this in my dreams—but I dreamed that I, quick to defiance and spurred on by anger, struck the ship's captain with another stone".'

ii

'Ek þóttumst úti staddr, ok sá ek konur tvær. Þær höfðu trog í milli sín, ok námu þær staðar á Hrísateigi ok jósu blóði um heraðit alt. Ok vaknaða ek síðan.'

'I thought I was outside and saw two women. They had a trough between them, and took up their places at Hrísateigr, and sprinkled blood over all the district. I afterwards awoke.'

P. 75. On his way home from the Althing at which he was
charged with the slaying of Þorvaldr krókr Þórisson, Glúmr had
the following dream:

...dreymdi hann at margir menn
væri komnir þar til Þverár at
hitta Frey, ok þóttist hann sjá
mart manna á eyrunum við ána,
enn Freyr sat á stóli. Hann
þóttist spyrja, hverir þar væri
komnir. Þeir segja: 'Þetta eru
frændr þínir framliðnir, ok bið-
jum vér nú Frey, at þú sér eigi
á brott færðr af Þverár-landi, ok
tjóar ekki, ok svarar Freyr stutt
ok reiðulega, ok minnist nú á
uxa-gjöf Þorkels ens háva'.

...he dreamed that many people
had come to Þverá to visit Freyr,
and that he saw many men on the
banks of the river, and Freyr
sitting on a throne. He thought
he asked who had come there.
They answered: 'We are your
departed relatives, and we are
petitioning Freyr that you be not
driven away from Þverá, but it is
no use, and Freyr answers shortly
and angrily; he remembers now
the gift of an ox made by Þorkell
enn hávi'.

Viga-Stýrs Saga ok Heiðarvíga.

P. 70. Before he was slain in a battle with his enemies,
Þorbjörn Brúnason had this dream:

'Þar þóttumst ek vera staddr, er
eigi þótti öllum einnug, ok þóttumst ek hafa sverðit þat, er ek
hefi vanr verit at hafa í hendi
mér, enn nú er eigi heima, ok
brotnaði í sundr, þegar ek hjó
fram; enn ek þóttumst kveða
vísur tvær í svefninum, ok man
ek þær báðar:

'I thought I was where men appeared not to be all of like mind,
and I thought I had the sword
which I have been accustomed to
have in my hand, but which is
now not at home. It broke
asunder as soon as I struck out
with it, and I thought I said two
verses in my sleep and I remember both of them:

"Þat varð mér at hinn mæra
(minn vandak brag) grandi
hjalm-Fenris brast holma
hvítvöndr í tvau rítar,
þars á mætu móti,
mótruðr jöru snótar,
heimþingaðar hanga
hnitu reyr saman dreyra.

"It befell that the glorious
gleaming sword broke asunder
in the fight. I compose my
verse with ease—where the
swords smote together in the
famous battle, warrior.

"Væri betr at bærak
benvönd í gný randa,

"It were better, man, if I carried
the blade noiseless in battle

hleypir kjóls, ok heilan
haus ókostalausan,
sás, dalreyðar, dauða,
dýrreitar, skal veita,
hirði-Baldr, ok heldim
hann ófðum manni."'

and my head whole, the one
which will give death to many,
man, and which I should hold
in my hand."'

P. 71. On the day that Barði Guðmundarson and his followers
came to attack them, Gísli Þorgautsson joined his brothers who
were mowing Gold-meadow, and recited this verse:

'Hér vildu mik höldar
húmfress í stað þessum
fálu fúra véla
fjölrœks marir sœkja
Hitt segir Ullr at allir
oddgaldrs munit skaldi
hríðar Hlakkar glóða
herðendr trúit verða.'

'Here in this place wolves
wanted to attack me; the careful warrior (I) was of good
courage; the warrior (I) says
that not all the warriors will
be faithful to the skald (me).'

Hann segir draum sinn, at honum
þótti sem þeir væri þar staddir á
Gullteig, ok kæmi at þeim vargar
margir, ok ættist þar við, ok var
mikit um—'ok ek þóttumst
vakna við þat, er ek hljóp undan
heim til bæjarins'.

He tells a dream of his in which
he thought they were standing on
Gold-meadow and many wolves
came upon them and dealt with
them, and there was a great
business of it—'and I thought I
wakened as I ran away home to
the stead'.

Völsunga Saga.

P. 61. Guðrún once dreamed thus of her future husband:

'Þat dreymde mik, at ek sa einn
fagran hauk mer a hende. Fiadrar
hans voru med gullighum lith.'

'I dreamed that I saw a beautiful
hawk on my arm, and his feathers
were the colour of gold.'

INDEX OF DREAMS

LIST OF WORKS CONSULTED

PRIMARY SOURCES

I. OLD NORSE LITERATURE

Áns Saga Bogsveigis. Fornaldarsögur Norðrlanda, ii (ed. V. Ásmundarson). Reykjavík, 1886.

Ásmundar Saga Kappabana. Fornaldarsögur Norðrlanda, ii (ed. V. Ásmundarson). Reykjavík, 1886.

Atlamöl en grønlenʒko. Die Lieder der Edda (ed. B. Sijmons). Halle, 1888.

Bárðar Saga Snæfellsáss (ed. V. Ásmundarson). Reykjavík, 1902.

Bjarnar Saga Hítdælakappa (ed. V. Ásmundarson). Reykjavík, 1898.

Egils Saga Skallagrímssonar (ed. V. Ásmundarson). Reykjavík, 1911.

Eireks Saga Víðförla. Fornaldarsögur Norðrlanda, iii (ed. V. Ásmundarson). Reykjavík, 1889.

Eiríks Saga Rauða (ed. B. Sveinsson). Reykjavík, 1926.

Eyrbyggja Saga (ed. B. Sveinsson). Reykjavík, 1921.

Færeyinga Saga (ed. Kongelige Nordiske Oldskriftselskab). Copenhagen, 1927.

Fagrskinna, Vols. i, ii (ed. F. Jónsson). Copenhagen, 1902–3.

Finnboga Saga (ed. B. Sveinsson). Reykjavík, 1922.

Fljótsdæla Saga (ed. B. Sveinsson). Reykjavík, 1921.

Flóamanna Saga (ed. B. Sveinsson). Reykjavík, 1926.

Fóstbræðra Saga (ed. V. Ásmundarson). Reykjavík, 1899.

Fóstbræðra Saga (ed. Björn K. Þorolfsson). Copenhagen, 1925–7.

Gísla Saga Súrssonar (ed. B. Sveinsson). Reykjavík, 1922.

Gunnlaugs Saga Ormstungu (ed. V. Ásmundarson). Reykjavík, 1911.

Guþrúnarkviþa. Die Lieder der Edda (ed. B. Sijmons). Halle, 1888.

Hallfreðar Saga (ed. V. Ásmundarson). Reykjavík, 1901.

Harðar Saga ok Hólmverja (ed. F. Jónsson). Reykjavík, 1908.
Hávarðar Saga Ísfirðings (ed. B. Sveinsson). Reykjavík, 1921.
Heimskringla. Snorri Sturluson (ed. F. Jónsson). Copenhagen, 1911.
Hervarar Saga ok Heiðreks. Fornaldarsögur Norðrlanda, I (ed. V. Ásmundarson). Reykjavík, 1891.
Hœnsa-þóris Saga (ed. F. Jónsson). Reykjavík, 1911.
Hrafnkels Saga Freysgoða (ed. V. Ásmundarson). Reykjavík, 1911.
Hrólfs Saga Gautrekssonar. Fornaldarsögur Norðrlanda, III (ed. V. Ásmundarson). Reykjavík, 1889.
Hrómundar Saga Greipssonar. Fornaldarsögur Norðrlanda, II (ed. V. Ásmundarson). Reykjavík, 1886.
Íslendingabók. Ari Þorgilsson (ed. V. Ásmundarson). Reykjavík, 1909.
Jómsvíkinga Saga. Fornmanna Sögur, 11 (ed. Norræna Fornfræða Félags). Copenhagen, 1828.
Jóns Saga hins Helga. Biskupa Sögur, I (ed. Íslenzka Bókmentafélagi). Copenhagen, 1858.
Kjalnesinga Saga (ed. V. Ásmundarson). Reykjavík, 1902.
Knytlínga Saga. Fornmanna Sögur, 11 (ed. Norræna Fornfræða Félags). Copenhagen, 1828.
Kormáks Saga (ed. B. Sveinsson). Reykjavík, 1916.
Landnámabók (ed. F. Jónsson). Copenhagen, 1900.
Laxdæla Saga (ed. B. Sveinsson). Reykjavík, 1920.
Ljósvetninga Saga (ed. B. Sveinsson). Reykjavík, 1921.
Morkinskinna (ed. F. Jónsson). Copenhagen, 1928–32.
Njáls Saga (ed. V. Ásmundarson). Reykjavík, 1910.
Orkneyinga Saga (ed. S. Nordal). Copenhagen, 1913–16.
Reykdæla Saga (ed. V. Ásmundarson). Reykjavík, 1897.
Saga Guðmundar Arasonar. Biskupa Sögur, I (ed. Íslenzka Bókmentafélagi). Copenhagen, 1858.
Saga Ólafs Konúngs Tryggvasonar. Fornmanna Sögur, I and 2 (ed. Norræna Fornfræða Félags). Copenhagen, 1825–6.
Skjaldedigtning, Vols. I, II (ed. F. Jónsson). Copenhagen, 1912–15.
Snorra Edda (ed. F. Jónsson). Reykjavík, 1907.

Sögubrot af Fornkonungum. *Fornaldarsögur Norðrlanda*, 1 (ed. V. Ásmundarson). Reykjavík, 1891.

Sögubrot um Jón Arason. *Biskupa Sögur*, 11 (ed. Íslenzka Bókmentafélagi). Copenhagen, 1858.

Sturlunga Saga, Vols. 1, 11 (ed. Kongelige Nordiske Oldskriftselskab). Copenhagen and Christiania, 1906–11.

Svarfdæla Saga (ed. V. Ásmundarson). Reykjavík, 1898.

Sverris Saga. Fornmanna Sögur, 8 (ed. Norræna Fornfræða Félags). Copenhagen, 1834.

þáttr af þorvaldi Viðförla. Biskupa Sögur, 1 (ed. Íslenzka Bókmentafélagi). Copenhagen, 1858.

þáttr Ólafs Geirstaða Álfs. Fornmanna Sögur, 10 (ed. Norræna Fornfræða Félags). Copenhagen, 1835.

þáttr Orms Stórólfssonar. Fornmanna Sögur, 3 (ed. Norræna Fornfræða Félags). Copenhagen, 1827.

þorfinns Saga Karlsefnis (ed. V. Ásmundarson). Reykjavík, 1902.

þórleifs þáttr Jarlsskálds. Fjörutíu Íslendinga þættir (ed. F. Jónsson). Reykjavík, 1904.

þorskfirðinga Saga (ed. V. Ásmundarson). Reykjavík, 1897.

þorsteins Saga Hvíta (ed. V. Ásmundarson). Reykjavík, 1902.

þorsteins Saga Síðu-Hallssonar (ed. V. Ásmundarson). Reykjavík, 1902.

þorsteins Saga Víkingssonar. Fornaldarsögur Norðrlanda, 11 (ed. V. Ásmundarson). Reykjavík, 1886.

þórsteins þáttr Uxafóts. Fjörutíu Íslendinga þættir (ed. F. Jónsson). Reykjavík, 1904.

þórðar Saga Hræðu (ed. V. Ásmundarson). Reykjavík, 1900.

Vafþrúþnesmöl. Die Lieder der Edda (ed. B. Sijmons). Halle, 1888.

Vápnfirðinga Saga (ed. V. Ásmundarson). Reykjavík, 1898.

Vatnsdæla Saga (ed. V. Ásmundarson). Reykjavík, 1913.

Vegtamskviþa. Die Lieder der Edda (ed. B. Sijmons). Halle, 1888.

Viga-Glúms Saga (ed. V. Ásmundarson). Reykjavík, 1897.

Viga-Stýrs Saga ok Heiðarvíga (ed. V. Ásmundarson). Reykjavík, 1899.

Víglundar Saga (ed. V. Ásmundarson). Reykjavík, 1902.

Völsunga Saga (ed. Magnus Olsen). Copenhagen, 1906.

II. FOLKLORE

Aberglaube und Sagen aus dem Herzogthum Oldenburg, No. 2
(ed. L. Strackerjan). Oldenburg, 1867.
Allmogeseder i Rönnebärgs Härad i Skåne (ed. E. Wigström).
De Svenska landsmal, Vol. VIII, 2. Stockholm, 1891.
Archiv for Skolevæsenet i Christiansand. Copenhagen, 1803.
Bidrag til Södermanlands äldre Kulturhistorie, Vol. VIII (ed. J.
Wahlfisk). Strangnäs, 1895.
County Folklore, Vol. III. *Orkney and Shetland Islands* (coll.
and ed. G. F. Black and N. W. Thomas). London, 1903.
Danmarks Gamle Folkeviser, Vols. I–VIII (ed. S. Grundtvig).
Copenhagen, 1853–1904.
Danske Folkeæventyr (ed. E. T. Kristensen). Viborg, 1888.
Danske Folkeæventyr, Vol. I (ed. S. Grundtvig). Copenhagen,
1876.
Danske Folkeminder (ed. J. Kamp). Odense, 1877.
Danske Ordsprog og Mundheld (ed. E. T. Kristensen). Copen-
hagen, 1890.
Danske Sagn, som de har lydt i folkemunde (ed. E. T. Kristensen).
Vols. I, II, Aarhus, 1892; III, Silkeborg, 1895; IV, Aarhus,
1896.
Det jyske almueliv, Vols. I–V (ed. E. T. Kristensen). Kolding
and Copenhagen, 1891–4.
Die Volkssagen Ostpreussens, Litthauens und Westpreussens (ed.
Tettau and Temme). Berlin, 1865.
Dulsýnir, Vols. I, II (ed. S. Sigfússon). Reykjavík, 1915 and
1930.
Færöske Folkesagn og Æventyr (ed. J. Jakobsen). Copenhagen,
1898–1901.
Folkevennen. Christiania, 1862.
Folkminner och Folktankar, Vols. I–IV (ed. C. v. Sydow).
Göteborg, 1927.
Fra Gammal Tid (ed. A. Rostad). *Norsk Folkeminnelag*, 25.
Oslo, 1931.
Fra Nordlands Fortid, No. 2. O. Nicolaissen. Christiania, 1891.
Gamalt fra Numedal, No. 3 (ed. T. Flatin).

Gamalt or Sætesdal, Nos. 3–5 (ed. J. Skar). Christiania, 1908–11.
Gamle Danske Minder, Nos. 1–3 (ed. S. Grundtvig). Copenhagen, 1854–61.
Gráskinna, Vols. I–III (ed. S. Nordal and Þ. Þórðarson). Akureyri, 1928–31.
Gríma. Þjóðsögur, Nos. I–IV (ed. O. Björnsson and J. Rafnar). Akureyri, 1929–31.
Historical Tales and Legends of the Highlands (ed. A. Mackenzie). Inverness, 1878.
Historie-gubbar fra Dal. A. Bondeson. Stockholm, 1886.
Historiske Fortællinger om Islændernes Færd, Vols. I–IV (ed. Kongelige Nordiske Oldskriftselskab). Copenhagen, 1839–44.
Hiterdals Beskrivelse. C. Glükstad. Christiania, 1878.
Hulder og Trollskap (ed. S. Nergaard). Norsk Folkeminnelag, 11. Oslo, 1925.
I Fjeldbygderne. P. Söegaard. Christiania, 1868.
Islendʒk Æventyri, Vols. I, II (ed. H. Gering). Halle, 1882–4.
Íslenʒk Fornkvæði, Vols. I, II (ed. S. Grundtvig and J. Sigurðsson). Copenhagen, 1854–8, 1859–85.
Íslenʒkar þjóðsögur og Sagnir, Vols. I–III (ed. S. Sigfússon). Seyðisfjörður, 1922–5.
Jul, Vols. I, II. F. H. Feilberg. Copenhagen, 1904.
Jydske Folkeminder, Vols. I–VI (ed. E. T. Kristensen). Copenhagen, 1871–83.
Kynnehuset (ed. P. Lunde). Norsk Folkeminnelag. Christiania, 1924.
Lappiske eventyr og folkesagn (ed. T. Qvigstad and G. Sandberg). Christiania, 1887.
Maal og Minne, Vols. I–IV (ed. M. Olsen). Oslo, 1926.
Maal og Minne, Vol. IV (ed. M. Olsen). Oslo, 1914.
Makter og Menneske (ed. H. Opedal). Norsk Folkeminnelag, 23. Oslo, 1930.
Nordiske Oldskrifter, Vols. XII, XX, XXVII (ed. Nordiske Literatur-Samfund). Copenhagen, 1851, 1855, 1860.
Norges Land og Folk. Jarlsberg og Larviks amt. Vol. II. A. Helland. Christiania, 1914.

Norsk Folkekultur. Christiania, 1924.
Norske Bygdemaal, Nos. 12–17. H. Ross. Christiania, 1909.
Norske Bygdesagn, No. 2. L. Daae. Christiania, 1872.
Norske Folke-Eventyr. 2nd ed. (ed. Asbjörnsen and Moe).
    Christiania, 1876.
Norske Folkesagn. 2nd ed. A. Faye. Christiania, 1844.
Norske Folkevisor, Vols. I–III (ed. K. Liestøl and M. Moe).
    Christiania, 1920–4.
Norske Huldre-eventyr og Norske Folke-eventyr, Vols. I–II (ed.
    Asbjörnsen and Moe). Christiania, 1914.
Norske Minnestykke. I. Aasen. *Norsk Folkeminnelag.* Chris-
    tiania, 1923.
Optegnelser paa Vendelbomaal. O. Grönborg. Copenhagen,
    1884.
Popular tales of the West Highlands, Vols. I–IV (ed. J. Campbell).
    Edinburgh, 1860–2.
Prophecies of the Brahan Seer (ed. A. Mackenzie). Inverness,
    1882.
Rauðskinna. J. Thorarensen. Reykjavík, 1929.
Sagen, Märchen und Gebräuche aus Meklenburg, Nos. 1 and 2
    (ed. K. Bartsch). Wien, 1879–80.
Sagnakver, Vol. II. B. Bjarnason. Ísafjörður, 1902.
Segner fra Sogn, No. 2. O. Sande. Bergen, 1892.
Skikk og Bruk (ed. S. Nergaard). *Norsk Folkeminnelag,* 16.
    Oslo, 1927.
Svartboka. K. Ostberg. Oslo, 1927.
Svenska Folkets Sago-Häfder, Vols. I–V (ed. A. Afzelius).
    Stockholm, 1839–43.
Þjóðsögur og Æfintýri, Vols. I, II, III (ed. J. Árnason). Reykjavík,
    1909, 1920, 1924.
Þjóðsögur og Munnmæli (ed. J. Þorkelsson). Reykjavík, 1899.
*The High Deeds of Finn, and other Bardic Romances of Ancient
    Ireland.* T. Rolleston. London, 1910.
Währen och Wirdarne, Vol. I. Hylten-Cavallius. Stockholm,
    1864.

SECONDARY SOURCES

CHADWICK, H. M. and N. K. *The Growth of Literature*, Vol. I. Cambridge, 1932.

CRAIGIE, W. A. *The Icelandic Sagas*. Cambridge, 1913.

EHRENSPERGER, E. C. *Dream Words in Old and Middle English*. Publications of the Modern Language Association, Vol. XLVI. New York, 1931.

FEILBERG, F. H. *Sjæletro*. Copenhagen, 1914.

HENZEN, W. *Über die Träume in der Altnordischen Sagalitteratur*. Leipzig, 1890.

HERMANNSSON, H. *Islandica*, Vols. III, XIX, XX, XXI. New York, 1910, 1929, 1930, 1931.

JÓNSSON, FINNUR. *Den Oldnorske og Oldislandske Litteraturs Historie*, Vols. I–III. Copenhagen, 1920–3.

LEACH, H. G. *Angevin Britain and Scandinavia*. Cambridge, 1921.

LIESTØL, K. *The origin of the Icelandic Family Sagas*. Oslo, 1930.

MACKENZIE, G. S. *Travels in Iceland*. Edinburgh, 1812.

MAURER, K. *Die Bekehrung des Norwegischen Stammes zum Christenthume*. München, 1855–6.

NERMAN, B. *The Poetic Edda in the Light of Archaeology*. Coventry, 1931.

PHILLPOTTS, B. S. *Edda and Saga*. Cambridge, 1931.

—— 'Germanic Heathenism.' *The Cambridge Medieval History*, Vol. II. Cambridge, 1913.

—— *Temple Administration and Chieftainship in Pre-Christian Norway and Iceland*. Reprint from the Saga Book of the Viking Club. London, 1914.

—— *The Elder Edda*. Cambridge, 1920.

—— 'Soul (Teutonic).' Hastings' *Encyclopædia of Religion and Ethics*, Vol. II.

—— *Wyrd and Providence in Anglo-Saxon Thought*. Essays and Studies of the English Association. Oxford, 1928.

REICHBORN-KJENNERUD, I. *Vår Gamle Trolldomsmedisin*. Oslo, 1928.

RIVERS, W. H. R. *The Symbolism of Rebirth.* Presidential Address to the Folk-Lore Society. 1922.

—— *Conflict and Dream.* London, 1923.

SAXO GRAMMATICUS. Latin History translated by O. Elton.

SHETELIG, H. *Préhistoire de la Norvège.* Oslo, 1926.

SPENCE, L. *An Introduction to Mythology.* London, 1921.

THORODDSSEN, T. *Islandsk Folketru.* Christiania, 1924.

DICTIONARIES

BLÖNDAL, S. *Islandsk-Dansk Ordbog.* Reykjavík, 1920–4.

EGILSSON, S. *Lexicon Poeticum* (ed. F. Jónsson). Copenhagen, 1913–16.

FUNK AND WAGNALL. *Standard Dictionary of the English Language.* New York and London, 1911.

LARSEN, H. *Dansk-Norsk-Engelsk Ordbog.* Copenhagen and Christiania, 1910.

ROSS, H. *Norsk Ordbog.* Christiania, 1895.

VIGFUSSON, G. *Icelandic-English Dictionary.* Oxford, 1874.

For EU product safety concerns, contact us at Calle de José Abascal, 56–1°,
28003 Madrid, Spain or eugpsr@cambridge.org.

www.ingramcontent.com/pod-product-compliance
Ingram Content Group UK Ltd.
Pitfield, Milton Keynes, MK11 3LW, UK
UKHW012340130625
459647UK00009B/430